A love affair with

PEONIES

A Love Affair with Peonies.
Published in Great Britain in 2022 by Bird Eye Books,
an imprint of Graffeg Limited.

Written by Alec White, copyright © 2023.
Designed and produced by Graffeg Limited,
copyright © 2023.

Graffeg Limited, 24 Stradey Park Business Centre,
Mwrwg Road, Llangennech, Llanelli, Carmarthenshire,
SA14 8YP, Wales, UK. www.graffeg.com.

The publisher gratefully acknowledges the financial
support of this book by the Books Council of Wales.
www.gwales.com.

ISBN 9781913733957

1 2 3 4 5 6 7 8 9

MIX
Paper from
responsible sources
FSC® C014138

Cover photo: *Paeonia* 'Scarlet O'Hara' AGM.
Photograph by Caron Saunders.

End paper: Early spring in the nursery.
© Richard Bloom.

Above: *Paeonia* 'Blushing Princess'.

Photo credits: All photos by Herbert White & Sons
Ltd except Clive Nichols (p.46-47, 67, 86, 91, 92, 93, 144),
Richard Bloom (title page, p.21, 110 *Paeonia* 'Garden
Treasure'), Paul Grover (p.172-173), Lauren Harper
(p.34, 45). Illustrations by Carolyn Carter (p.142-143).

Primrose Hall Peonies, Bedfordshire
www.primrosehallpeonies.co.uk

A love affair with

PEONIES

Alec White

Dedicated to my grandparents,
who instilled their love of plants in me.

BIRD EYE BOOKS

Preface

There are many reasons to fall in love with peonies; they are well known for their aesthetic qualities, with decadent and exquisite blooms that command attention in an astonishing range of colours and sizes and beautiful fragrances.

This book is about my experience of growing peonies; it is not a definitive treatise. I don't consider myself an expert – I am entirely self-taught and on a journey of discovery as I pursue my passion for peonies.

There are many reasons to fall in love with peonies; they are well known for their aesthetic qualities, with decadent and exquisite blooms that command attention in an astonishing range of colours and sizes and beautiful fragrances. Even at the end of each season, in their dying days, with wonderful foliage and seedpods, peonies are a powerful presence in the garden, displaying grace and beauty. For me, one of their key qualities is that they are so easy to grow. They may look delicate and fragile, and each plant may only flower for a few weeks each year, but they are incredibly robust and long-lived and require very little care and maintenance. This means that they are resilient, and with a small garden, three young children and a very energetic dog (Mallory), this is absolutely crucial for me. To survive there, plants must be able to cope with minimal care and be tough enough to withstand the dog running through them and footballs (and occasionally small children) landing on them. In many respects, therefore, peonies are perfect plants for all gardeners, whether you are a beginner or a more experienced horticulturist.

I speak to thousands of people each year at flower shows and it is clear that peonies are well loved; everyone seems to have a peony story of their own. Being such a long-lived plant, perhaps it is no surprise that peonies have the capacity to hold so many memories, and I am often told of the connection they have to childhood or loved ones.

Above: Primrose Hall Peonies RHS Gold Medal 2019.

Left: Taking out side shoots to produce larger single flowers in early season.

Left: *Paeonia x festiva* 'Rubra Plena' AGM.

Right: *Paeonia lactiflora* 'Sarah Bernhardt' AGM, photographed at National Trust property Woburn Abbey and Gardens, Bedfordshire.

I have lost count of the times I've been told that peonies featured in bridal bouquets and how a peony plant reminds a couple of their special day. However, there is often a note of disappointment when people describe their peony experiences: 'They don't flower for very long, do they?', or 'Peonies are lovely, but very difficult to grow', or 'My peony doesn't flower any longer', or 'I had a beautiful peony, but when we moved house I had to leave it behind – they don't like being moved, do they?'

In this book I hope to dispel some of these myths and provide inspiration and encouragement to others to become more confident about growing peonies.

Alec White

Contents

At the outset I was pretty clear about how I wanted this book to be: easy to read, interesting and informative, fun and entertaining, full of beautiful photographs, accessible to both gardeners and non-gardeners, encouraging and inspiring. Through these chapters I share my experience and knowledge of growing peonies and my story of pursuing my dream to run a peony nursery and exhibit at the highest level.

Peonies as Cut Flowers 123

Strong-stemmed, tall and with a vase life of seven to ten days, peonies make excellent cut flowers, allowing you to further experience, admire and enjoy them.

Fabulous Peony Flowers 135

Vibrant and decadent, peony blooms are undoubtedly their most show-stopping characteristic.

The Perfume of Peonies 151

While most well known for their visual qualities, peonies also offer a remarkable range of scents.

Common Myths about Peonies 159

Dispelling common peony myths and frequently asked questions to help your plants succeed.

The Stars of the Show 169

A behind-the-scenes look at the creativity and dedication required to exhibit and win awards at the UK's most prestigious flower shows.

Propagation 185

Learn the process of effectively dividing your peony roots or propagating from seed.

The Peony in Art and Culture 191

Discover the cultural significance the peony has maintained and its inclusion in art and literature around the world through the centuries.

Places to See Peonies 202

Where to find the finest peonies in the UK's public gardens.

My Love Affair with Peonies

I can say, hand on heart, that what initially attracted me to growing peonies was the sheer size and beauty of the blooms. I had never seen anything like it.

Why I love peonies

I can say, hand on heart, that what initially attracted me to growing peonies was the sheer size and beauty of the blooms. I had never seen anything like it.

In early summer 2007, the lengths of the stock beds in the nursery were full of various herbaceous perennial plants, a couple of thousand of them in row upon row. They were in early summer flower and featured every colour you can think of: pink, white, purple and mauve, blue, orange and yellow. It was a very pretty and quintessentially English cottage garden vista.

What caught my eye, though, were two huge, magnificent, fully double flowers. The blooms stood tall above most of the other perennials and had a gravitas about them, one a silky dark red and the other a magical puff of creamy white with a crimson edge on some of the petals. They weren't waving in the breeze or mingling with other flowers but were proud and dominant, seeming to own the space around them, set apart from the other perennials. I was mesmerised.

These two peonies, *Paeonia lactiflora* 'Peter Brand' and *Paeonia lactiflora* 'Festiva Maxima' AGM, captured my heart and imagination. 'Peter Brand' is perhaps one of the darkest red double-flowered peonies, while 'Festiva Maxima' is one of the largest double-flowered creamy white peonies. At the time, the plants were not particularly well established – they were container-grown plants on my nursery – and as soon as the blooms opened it seemed as if they had gone again and I was left waiting another year. I had no idea that peonies could be fragrant, that they could flower in the garden for more than a week or two, or of the range of colours or flower types they exhibit. All I knew at the time was that these plants appeared to stand head and shoulders above the other perennials in the nursery bed.

Left: *Paeonia lactiflora* 'Bowl of Beauty' looking magnificent in a mixed herbaceous border at Docwra's Manor Garden, Cambridgeshire.

As I have grown more and more cultivars, branching out into woody (also known as tree peonies) and intersectional peonies, and as my interest and passion has developed, the question of why I love them has become considerably more complex. I love that they are ancient survivors, hardy and long lived, and that there is still so much about them yet to be understood. I love that peonies are fragrant and make wonderful cut flowers in the home. I love the intricacies and technical endeavour that goes into researching and breeding new hybrids. I love that peonies are very low maintenance and rarely suffer from pests or diseases. But perhaps most of all I am still besotted with their magnificent blooms, in different shapes, sizes and colours.

My journey into horticulture

Though my love affair with peonies started around fifteen years ago, shortly after my parents and I bought the nursery, my love of gardening began long before that.

I have always loved being outdoors, playing and exploring, and much of my early childhood was spent in the garden with my cousins, often outside all day, left to our own devices. One of my earliest gardening memories is of being in my paternal grandparent's well-maintained garden and watching my grandad tending to his prize chrysanthemums. At the rear there was an allotment patch where he grew vegetables, flowers and soft fruit. My grandad would cover the chrysanthemum blooms in paper bags to protect them and strangely curl the petals with a pencil to achieve a perfect, uniform appearance for exhibition.

At about seven or eight years old and having pestered my parents for months about getting a greenhouse for our garden, they eventually relented and erected an 8' x 6' greenhouse for me. With a small allotment patch, my grandad began my gardening education. We started with tomatoes and the discipline of pinching out the side shoots, feeding and watering. Although I didn't actually like eating the tomatoes, I was fascinated watching them grow.

My love affair with peonies started around fifteen years ago, shortly after my parents and I bought the nursery, but my love of gardening started long before that.

Right: Holding an intersectional peony and looking at the juvenile blooms of *Paeonia* 'Love Affair' on the nursery on a beautiful day in early summer.

Top left: *Paeonia* 'Love Affair' before it has fully opened – one of my favourite intersectional hybrid peonies.

Top right: *Paeonia* 'First Arrival' AGM looking magnificent. I find this intersectional hybrid peony reliably produces masses of flowers each year.

Bottom left: *Paeonia lactiflora* 'Germaine Bigot', a gorgeous double flowering peony with light pink flowers.

Bottom right: *Paeonia lactiflora* 'Sebastian Maas'.

Page 18: Unknown variety of tree peony photographed at Highfield House, Derbyshire.

Page 19: *Paeonia delavayi* pictured at Highfield House, Derbyshire.

My annual seed order was a highlight, taking months of planning, and it wasn't long before I dabbled with bedding plants from seed, along with carrots, beetroots, potatoes and, one year, celery (although it didn't work out that well, if I recall correctly). I loved tending to my plants and would spend hours at the weekend and after school in the greenhouse. I eventually tried my hand at growing some exhibition chrysanthemums – some reflex and some incurve varieties. I spent a great deal of time on them, under the attentive and careful eye of my grandad, and, when the time came, entered them in the local flower show. Apparently, I was too young to enter the adult class for competition, but I did anyway, and it worked: I won first prize. It was my first exhibition entry, and, at the time, I had no idea I would one day exhibit at RHS Chelsea Flower Show and win a Gold Medal.

Junior school

I also remember being at junior school at around the same time and growing cress on some wet tissue paper in the classroom. I was clearly very interested in gardening because I remember asking if I could dig up some of the school playing field to grow vegetables. Unsurprisingly, I wasn't allowed to dig up the football pitch (I have never been particularly interested in football), but my teacher was sufficiently impressed and keen to support me and so I was given a small area outside the classroom that enabled me and a few friends to grow some runner beans and other vegetable plants.

My grandparents, both maternal and paternal, have always been supportive and encouraging of my love of gardening, and I think that is down to them and the hours and hours spent passing on knowledge and simply being together in the garden. It may be in my genes, though, as apparently my great-great-grandparents on both sides were market gardeners, so it is perhaps no surprise that I ended up in commercial horticulture. I am simply following a family tradition.

My first gardening job

As a twelve-year-old, I, like many of my school friends, was looking to earn some pocket money. I didn't much fancy getting up early and doing a paper round, and working in a shop didn't hold a great deal of appeal either. I decided that a Saturday job at the local garden centre and nursery (a few hundred metres from where we lived) would be ideal and very convenient. It took a while for the owner to agree to employ me – I seem to recall I had to visit several times before they eventually gave in and said I could water the hanging baskets after school a couple of times a week. That decision changed my life.

I would get thoroughly soaked each time watering the hanging baskets (there were about 3,000 of them in total) and soon learnt the importance of careful and proper watering after having nearly wiped out the entire crop of fuchsia baskets through overwatering. In time I would assist in a range of nursery tasks, including feeding, potting, taking cuttings, pruning roses and cutting back perennials, and I loved every second of it. I was particularly fortunate because the owners had trained at the Royal Botanic Gardens, Kew, were very knowledgeable and patient and keen to explain and educate. I worked weekends and holidays there until I was about nineteen, travelling home at weekends whilst studying at university. From an early age I learnt that horticulture is pretty demanding, and whilst my friends were meeting up and hanging around town at the weekends I was at the nursery, watering and weeding. Horticulture is not for the faint-hearted, cold in the winter and hot in the summer in the greenhouses, and you have to be pretty determined. Regardless of your social calendar, the plants need care and attention.

I must have been about fifteen years old when my grandmother suggested we go to RHS Hampton Court Palace Flower Show. I can still remember our visit being on a very long, tiring, hot and sunny day. I was exhausted by the time we got home, but I had been inspired and captivated by the plants and show gardens and this started a tradition; for several years thereafter my grandmother and I would visit the Flower

From an early age I learnt that horticulture is pretty demanding, and whilst my friends were meeting up and hanging around town at the weekends, I was at the nursery, watering and weeding.

Right: Working in the nursery in mid-spring.
© Richard Bloom.

> *I remember talking with the careers advisor about my plans and being told that it was not the best course for me and that I wouldn't earn a sensible living working in horticulture.*

Show and make a real day of it, indulging our passion. I could not even imagine that one day I would be invited to exhibit my plants..

A career in horticulture

At the age of sixteen I was obliged to take careers advice and decide on which A-level courses to study. I was pretty clear that I wanted to study horticulture at Kew and follow in the footsteps of my mentors at the garden centre. I remember talking with the careers advisor about my plans and being told that it was not the best course for me and that I wouldn't earn a sensible living working in horticulture. I didn't really understand the argument, because as far as I could tell the owners of the garden centre and nursery I worked at seemed to be happy and enjoying a reasonable lifestyle. In any event, I was persuaded to study more academic subjects with a view to becoming a lawyer (I enjoyed a good argument, so this kind of made sense). The pathway to a career in horticulture for me was therefore circuitous. I studied law at university, got a master's degree in corporate law and was admitted to the bar. My career as a lawyer was, however, short and sweet. I very much enjoyed working in the magistrates' court, especially the sense of family that exists, and I made some really good friends along the way, but the fact is that it really wasn't what I wanted to do. So when the opportunity arose to follow my dreams, I did. In 2006 my parents and I purchased a nursery, about eight acres on a sloping site with good soil, surrounded by agricultural land and with incredible views of the landscape in beautiful, rural Bedfordshire.

Consequently, I didn't come to commercial horticulture with any formal training or qualifications; I've always relied on good observational skills, an enquiring mind and being able to ask others for technical help (which I have found has usually been very forthcoming). Having an interest in and a love for plants makes the journey so much more enjoyable and I have learnt a lot about peonies simply by growing lots of them.

Left: *Paeonia officinalis* 'Anemoniflora Rosea' AGM looking spectacular in the nursery growing tunnels.

The nursery

When we bought the nursery it was a small retail operation growing summer bedding that would be sold in a small farm shop and on the car park. Bedding plants have fallen out of favour a little in recent years and I don't see as many large-scale municipal planting schemes as I used to, which is a shame, because the vibrancy and eye-catching nature of bedding means that it brings a great deal of joy and beauty to all that pass by. I quickly found, though, that growing bedding is tough. Although it generally grows quite soon, it does require a lot of care, and a hard frost, if it catches you unawares, can quickly wipe out an entire crop. I therefore decided to experiment with growing perennial and alpine plants, which proved fascinating and provided a real education for me, and it was whilst growing herbaceous perennial plants that I came across peonies. From that moment on, I decided to concentrate solely on two crops: alstroemeria and peonies (alstroemeria are beautiful plants that, unlike peonies, flower for months on end and last for weeks as a cut flower indoors). Primrose Hall Peonies is now a specialist peony nursery with around 50-60,000 peonies in various stages of production at any one time, some in the ground (we have fairly decent, free-draining clay soil for the most part, although there are parts of the farm that are not so well drained) and the majority in containers. I am particularly interested in intersectional hybrid peonies and hold a National Collection.

I therefore decided to experiment with growing perennial and alpine plants, which proved fascinating and provided a real education for me.

Top left: Sun setting over the nursery in early summer.

Top right: Autumn planting in the peony field with bare-root peonies.

Bottom left: Potted plants providing excitement early in the season with jewel-like bright pink buds.

Bottom right: Plants in production.

Wildlife at the nursery

With a lot of wildlife on and around the nursery, it's fortunate that peonies are resistant to rabbits and deer, of which we have two types, Chinese water deer and muntjac deer, as well as voles, badgers, foxes, pheasants, partridges and populations of toads and newts. Nesting skylarks, swallows, falcons, buzzards and red kites swirl in the sky above us and lots of pollinators visit the nursery. It can be a busy place but the wildlife does not usually present us with any difficulties and generally works in harmony, making a healthy, inspiring and pleasant place to be.

As a nurseryman I am acutely aware of the effects of a changing climate and we try to work in a positive, sustainable way to protect and promote the countryside around us and mitigate our impact on the wider environment. The importance of the environment, strong rural economies and the essential role that plants have in creating a vibrant, healthy and beautiful planet is something that is close to my heart.

It may be a bit overenthusiastic to say, but maybe peonies, as long-lived plants, can contribute to carbon reduction and are a sensible choice for the garden particularly because they will tolerate the changing climate we face with warmer, drier summers and colder winters.

One of the measures we have deployed is a clowder of feral cats that live on site and patrol together to keep the area clear of rodents. We have chickens that we send into the field beds to fertilise the ground and reduce the slug and snail populations (and, of course, produce delicious eggs). In late 2020 we welcomed four alpacas to the nursery, and these provide us with a sustainable source of low-nutrient, slow-release pelleted fertiliser that we apply to our field-grown peonies (they are also great characters to have around the place and tend to deter the foxes from the chickens).

Top left: Muntjac deer, one of two types on the nursery.

Top right: Chickens amongst the peony beds.

Bottom left: Francesca, one of our herd of alpacas.

Bottom right: Common newts, further residents on the nursery.

Page 28-29: A well-established intersectional peony, with yellow blooms and dark green foliage, thriving next to swathes of hostas at Hodnet Hall, Shropshire.

Perfect Plants for the Garden

Undemanding, reliable and easy to grow, peonies are perhaps the perfect plant for the garden.

One of the interesting things I have learnt about peonies is that they are pretty hardy garden plants, making them perfect for gardeners of all abilities.

Peonies are long lived (I have been told by people that they have peony plants in their gardens that are over 100 years old) and usually require little maintenance or care, being pretty drought tolerant in the summer and not minding the harshest English winters. Of course, they also have the most stunning selection of flower blooms. As peony plants mature and settle into their long life, they will often produce more and more blooms each year, providing an abundance of flowers. As a result of their longevity, peonies can be considered inheritance plants that can be passed from one generation to another, hopefully inspiring the next crop of gardeners along the way and carrying memories and cherished thoughts with them. Peonies may be a little more expensive to purchase than some other more short-lived perennial plants, but when looked at over their lifetime they are actually very cost effective and provide exceptional value for money. Undemanding, reliable and easy to grow, peonies are perhaps the perfect plant for the garden.

Selecting peonies

Choosing the perfect peony for your own garden, however, is more complicated, given the wide range of cultivars and species available, and there is a real risk that you can become addicted to collecting peonies. This isn't a bad thing, but unless you have a very large garden you will have to choose carefully. In my very small courtyard garden at home, we have a lot of peonies and a lot of roses; they make a simple yet fine pairing, as the roses will flower for most of the summer. Winter colour in my garden depends on my flowering cherry tree and some evergreen hedging that the birds adore for shelter.

Left: *Paeonia* 'Court Jester', a striking and wonderful intersectional hybrid peony.

There are various factors to consider when choosing peonies, and I will look at many of these in more detail later in this book. Selecting the best possible peony varieties or cultivars for your intended use or particular garden conditions will ensure that you have success and get the most out of your peonies. For example, consider factors such as flower size, flower shape, flower colour and flowering time, fragrance, position within the garden, habit and shape, foliage, and whether you wish to grow peonies for use as a cut flower. Factors such as stem strength, resistance to disease, reliability, general vigour and wealth of blooms are also equally important to making a good selection for cut flower production. For now, note only that peonies require a cold period each winter to initiate flower buds to produce the best results, together with fertile, free-draining soil.

When selecting peonies, you may choose to look through supplier catalogues or use the Internet, but possibly one of the better ways is to visit gardens (whether those that are owned by friends and family or those that are open to the public) and observe the plants in person, which will give a far better idea of the plant's growth habit and flowering. We open our nursery each year and invite members of the public to view the peonies in production and in our trial beds, which is a good way to look at many different cultivars and compare them. Our open days are usually great fun, with talks, tours, tea and cakes, and the whole team really looks forward to them. It is wonderful to be able to show off our peonies and talk to other like-minded people that are passionate about peonies too!

AGM: What does it mean?

The Royal Horticultural Society Award of Garden Merit (AGM) is awarded to plants that the RHS expert panels have determined have outstanding performance in the garden. Herbaceous peonies have recently been trialled by the RHS (2016-2020), resulting in in excess of fifty peonies being awarded the AGM. There are many excellent peony cultivars and species to choose from, and looking at those that have been awarded the AGM may be a good place to start when selecting peonies for your collection.

When selecting peonies you may choose to look through supplier catalogues or use the Internet but possibly one of the better ways is to visit gardens.

Right: *Paeonia lactiflora* 'Sarah Berhardt' AGM, a beautiful pink double peony at National Trust property Osterley Park and House, London.

Types of Peonies

Intersectional or Itoh peonies are a cross between woody and herbaceous peonies.

There are species, herbaceous, woody and intersectional peonies to choose from, each with different growth habits.

Herbaceous or border peonies

Most people know the herbaceous or border peonies, in particular the cottage garden favourite, *Paeonia x festiva* 'Rubra Plena' AGM, the peony grandma had in her garden for years: bright red, masses of flowers, reasonably compact and virtually indestructible. Indeed, one of the most popular herbaceous peonies is *Paeonia lactiflora* 'Sarah Bernhardt' AGM, a fragrant, gorgeous pink bloom with a crimson edge. Equally well known is *Paeonia lactiflora* 'Bowl of Beauty' (cerise pink with a cream, spidery centre), which is both beautiful and incredibly reliable. Herbaceous peonies will grow to varying heights, from a compact 30-40cm up to around 1.2m (although more usually around 90cm), dying off completely in the autumn and returning again the following spring.

Woody or tree peonies

Woody or tree peonies are also common in gardens, although they are not at all 'trees'. Woody stemmed and growing between 1.2m and 2.1m tall with enormous flowers, woody peonies make excellent garden shrubs, are easily recognisable and hard to forget (especially varieties such as *Paeonia suffruticosa* 'Renkaku', which has heavenly white, lightly scented flowers the size of dinner plates, or *Paeonia ludlowii*, with its bright, golden-yellow cupped flowers). Woody peonies generally tend to flower earlier in the season and although they will lose their leaves in the autumn, their woody stems will remain through the winter.

Intersectional or Itoh peonies

Intersectional (sometimes called 'Itoh') peonies are a cross between woody and herbaceous peonies, in many respects providing the best of both to create an excellent garden plant. Itoh peonies are named after Toichi Itoh, a Japanese breeder who in the late 1940s succeeded in hybridising a herbaceous peony with a woody peony to create a plant with the best characteristics of both. Sadly, Toichi Itoh died before he ever

Left: *Paeonia* 'Pastel Splendor', a stunning intersectional peony pictured on the nursery in Bedfordshire, England. Photograph by Lauren Harper.

Herbaceous Peonies

Paeonia lactiflora 'Garden Lace' – Herbaceous peony

Paeonia lactiflora 'Kansas' AGM – Herbaceous peony

Paeonia lactiflora 'Bowl of Beauty' – Herbaceous peony

Paeonia lactiflora 'Candy Stripe' – Herbaceous peony

Paeonia suffruticosa 'Fuso no tsukasa' – Tree peony

Paeonia suffruticosa 'Okan' – Tree peony

Paeonia suffruticosa 'Koki-Jishi' – Tree peony

Paeonia suffruticosa 'Teikan' – Tree peony

saw his new hybrids flower, however, since the first hybrids appeared in the mid-1970s, breeders have been working hard to introduce new cultivars and the range of intersectional peonies has steadily increased.

Intersectional peonies are compact (but often substantial) plants (usually around 2'6"-3' high) that die down completely in the winter before emerging again in the spring. So far this sounds very similar to a herbaceous peony, but an intersectional hybrid has masses of much larger flowers and, because of its woody peony heritage, it generally does not require any staking to support their weight. Generally speaking, intersectional peonies flower for longer than both herbaceous and woody peonies, sometimes for four to five weeks in early to mid-season, and when mature can easily have fifty or sixty blooms or more on each plant. Intersectional peonies also have stunning finely cut foliage that looks great throughout the summer, with a red tinge in spring and showing a kaleidoscope of colour in early autumn.

Peonies are well known for their big, blousy, sumptuous flowers and intersectional peonies take this a step further with an incredible range of shapes, colours and colour combinations. Just look at *Paeonia* 'Lollipop', for example – it has unbelievably bright yellow flowers with purple flecks, making this a really striking peony. For something to really catch the eye, *Paeonia* 'Morning Lilac' AGM stands out, with its bright purple flowers and golden stamens. If it's pastels you need, how about *Paeonia* 'Pastel Splendor', which has gorgeous semi-double flowers that are lavender and pale pink with a deeper burgundy flare from the centre; the seed head on this cultivar is also worthy of note. *Paeonia* 'Court Jester' has a different flower shape entirely; it is a single flower with petals shaped like a jester's hat and golden yellow flowers with strong burgundy basal flares and orange stamens in the centre. The semi-double flowers of *Paeonia* 'Julia Rose' open a dark cerise pink, becoming cream with raspberry stripes as it matures and ultimately the entire flower turns creamy white. *Paeonia* 'Cora Louise' AGM is a beautiful pale lavender with darker purple flares from the centre; the flowers can be 10" across and are lightly fragrant, making 'Cora Louise' truly special.

Intersectional peonies are compact plants that die down completely in the winter before emerging again in the spring.

Paeonia 'Sonoma Floozy' – Intersectional peony

Paeonia 'Sonoma Amethyst' – Intersectional peony

Paeonia 'Julia Rose' – Intersectional peony

Paeonia 'Lollipop' – Intersectional peony

The plant's own food reserves will sustain it and with very little care it will live for many decades.

The importance of good roots

The most important consideration when purchasing a peony is the maturity of the plant, and more precisely the maturity of the roots, because peonies often don't tend to flower reliably until they are five or more years old. At five years and over, the peony roots will have three to five or more buds (or 'eyes') and will be much more resilient and likely to flower the following season. As seedlings, peonies are vulnerable to pests and diseases and inherently more delicate and susceptible to the worst ravages of nature. Once the plant matures and the tuberous roots develop, though, peonies quickly become robust, especially with fat, healthy, roots that store food to keep the plant going through the winter and other tough times. If the plant does not get sufficient food and nutrients in the growing season, it will eventually deplete its own food reserves and die. Usually, though, the plant's own food reserves will sustain it and with very little care it will live for many decades. The importance of strong, healthy roots cannot be understated.

The importance of good root systems applies equally to herbaceous and woody peonies, but perhaps even more so to woody peonies because many of the plants that are available in the garden centre will have been grafted onto herbaceous root stock in order to produce a commercially viable plant more quickly. There are advantages and disadvantages to 'own root' and grafted woody peonies, but ultimately both will provide healthy plants if cared for properly.

Woody peonies with their 'own roots' often take longer to establish, being especially vulnerable during their first few years in the garden, but will eventually produce a better, stronger plant.

Far left: Two-year-old tree peony grafted onto rootstock.

Left top: Herbaceous peony bare root showing the crown and bright pink, jewel-like buds (or 'eyes').

Left bottom: Herbaceous bare-root peony showing fine white hairy feeder roots.

Grafted woody peonies

Grafted woody peonies will often establish more quickly in the garden because the woody peony stem is joined to the roots of a mature herbaceous peony (known as a nurse root) and, of course, grafting enables the nurseryman to produce many more plants. Over time, the woody peony will produce its own roots and become less reliant on the nurse root. One of the main problems with grafted woody peonies is that sometimes the nurse root will start to produce its own growth (often known as 'suckers'), which will compete with the woody peony for food and nutrients and, if left, will eventually kill the woody peony. To mitigate this risk, grafted peonies should be planted deeper than herbaceous peonies.

The most important thing to know when planting grafted peonies is that the graft union (where the top part of the woody peony is joined to the roots) should be planted at least 4-6" below the soil surface. This will discourage the nurse root from sending up herbaceous shoots and encourage the woody peony to create its own root system to rely on.

Species peonies

Species peonies are those peonies that are wildflowers, native to various parts of the Northern Hemisphere and not the result of human interference and breeding. There is some debate about exactly how many species there actually are, but it's around thirty-three. Species peonies are of vital importance in terms of their genetic diversity and contribution to local ecological systems and habitats; this means that their wide gene pool is also crucial for future breeding of new cultivars of peonies. However, the number of species is under threat (and has been for some time) because of habitat destruction, with many species facing extinction in the wild. The flowers of species peonies are often smaller and more delicate and, because of the wide range of habitats they are native to, they have different habits, flowers and foliage to suit their environment, from open woodland to rocky, mountainous terrain, meaning that species peonies are often terribly interesting and charming.

Top left: *Paeonia emodi* AGM.

Top right: *Paeonia corsica*.

Bottom left: *Paeonia tenuifolia* 'Rubra Plena'.

Bottom right: *Paeonia delavayi*.

Bare-root or potted peonies?

Buying bare-root peonies can be a really cost-effective way to increase your peony collection. It is important to purchase good-quality bare roots if you want to have successful and healthy plants, and this means buying from a reputable peony nursery.

So often bare-root peony plants are offered for sale on general perennial websites which are of poor quality but an attractive low price, and when the plant fails to flourish, gardeners may question whether it is their actions or skill or whether in fact peonies are just tricky plants to grow when in reality the reason for the failure of the plant is neither. Bare roots are lifted in the early autumn and ideally should be planted as quickly as possible, certainly before the end of the autumn, to ensure they are as healthy and strong as possible. Although peony bare roots can be kept in cold storage, they do deteriorate and I would not recommend purchasing bare roots in the spring or summer, by which time they will have been kept in cold storage for too long. When buying bare-root peonies, try to ensure that they have at least between three and five buds (or 'eyes'), avoiding those that have any sign of damage – these plants will be more likely to thrive in your garden. The tubers should be firm (not rotten, hollow or squishy) and be free from lumps, bumps or mildew.

Interesting foliage

Given the wide distribution of peony species around the world and how they have adapted to different climates, it is perhaps no surprise that peonies can have such different and distinctive foliage. The contrast can be quite arresting; for example, *Paeonia tenuifolia* has very fine, fern-like, pale green leaves whereas *Paeonia lactiflora* has much broader, larger, dark glossy green leaves. The foliage can be very interesting and even architectural in the border, providing variation and relief. With differing shades of green in the spring and summer to a riot of colour in the autumn, the foliage can provide interest throughout the year and should not be overlooked.

Bare roots are lifted in the early autumn and ideally should be planted as quickly as possible, certainly before the end of the autumn, to ensure they are as healthy and strong as possible.

Above: Potted intersectional (left), woody (centre) and herbaceous peonies (right).

Bottom left: Alec showing visitors around the nursery on one of our open days. Photograph by Lauren Harper.

Bottom right: Examples of the different leaf shapes that peonies have.

Pages 46-47: Pink peonies in a cutting garden, Ven House, Somerset. © Clive Nichols.

Above: *Paeonia* 'Walter Mains'.

Top left: New buds forming in early spring.

Top right: *Paeonia* 'Scarlet O'Hara' AGM.

Bottom left: Potted peonies on a sales bench, RHS Garden Wisley.

Bottom right: Potted peonies in production on the nursery.

Pages 50-51: Large mixed border with peonies, Osterley Park and House, London.

Potted peonies

The alternative is to purchase a potted peony that may be a little more costly initially but will have the added benefit of being properly planted and have a well-developed root system, meaning it will become established sooner in your garden and potentially bloom more quickly. Often, peonies purchased in containers will come with a plant guarantee for added reassurance and confidence.

Peonies do not generally tend to flower reliably until they are at least five years old (with woody peonies it can be seven to eight years old), so look for mature, well-established plants. The additional cost may be questioned, but when the cost of plants purchased for the garden are added up over the years, there are few plants to compare with the value for money a peony provides because of its extreme longevity, ease of flowering, hardiness and low maintenance requirement.

Growing and Caring for Peonies

Patience and observation are key skills for any gardener, but perhaps especially so for those growing peonies.

The fleeting elegance of the peony's big, blousy blooms in summer may lead some gardeners to think that peonies are delicate and difficult to grow.

Patience and observation are key skills for any gardener, but perhaps especially so for those growing peonies. Peonies grow slowly, taking time to produce sufficient root systems to enable them to be divided, and they flower only once each year, so patience is essential; any short-term frustrations must be weighed against the longevity of the plant, which will continue to make steady progress for many decades. Observation is always important in the garden and with peonies a careful eye must be kept on the growth of nearby shrubs and trees to ensure the peony is not deprived of sufficient light to enable it to flower. Actually, peonies are quite easy to grow and are undemanding and very low maintenance provided you follow some basic rules at the outset.

Four simple rules for growing peonies

1. Plant a mature peony – this will mean that the chance of the plant establishing will be increased.

2. Plant peonies in full sun or part shade.

3. Plant peonies in any fertile, free-draining soil.

4. Plant peonies at the correct depth – herbaceous and intersectional peonies should not be planted with the crown more than 2.5-5cm below the soil surface. Woody peonies (and especially those that have been grafted) should be planted around 10-15cm below the soil surface.

Left: Beautiful peonies in a large border at Hodnet Hall, Shropshire.

A well-established peony that has been correctly planted in suitable soil and with sufficient light levels is unlikely to demand very much maintenance at all throughout its usually very long life and will happily produce an increasing number of magnificent flowers each year.

Location

When planting peonies, first consider the location. Peonies prefer plenty of space around them, so think about whether the peony is free from the risk of overcrowding from other plants. Remember that the peony will likely be in place for several decades and therefore could become crowded by what currently may be small trees or shrubs which will grow in time. Generally speaking, herbaceous peonies do best in a more sheltered position; wind and extreme weather can demolish flower blooms. Woody peonies and intersectional peonies will tolerate a more exposed position but will often grow to become more substantial plants requiring a little more space. Peonies can be used in the border as part of a planting scheme or as a focal point, a specimen planted to show off the peony in all its glory. Finally, remember to plant the peony somewhere it can be seen and appreciated, especially if it has a fragrance.

Planting in containers

Peonies tend to perform best when planted in the ground and will happily stay put in the same place for decades. If you have a smaller garden or a balcony, there are some more compact peonies that will do well for a period (perhaps three or four years) in a suitably large container. Look for shorter, more compact varieties, as taller varieties, often used for cut flowers, can be top-heavy and topple a container. The intersectional hybrids are often good candidates for containers because of their compact habit not requiring staking and their hugely floriferous nature.

Planting in containers will require you to ensure that there is good drainage in the pot and regular watering and feeding are a must. Though the plants will ultimately be happier in the ground, for a few years at least peonies in containers can give colour and joy.

When planting peonies, first consider the location. Peonies prefer plenty of space around them.

Right: Freshly planted peonies in the field in the autumn. Our field is well drained and open despite being clay-based.

The suitability of the local soil conditions is of paramount importance when planting peonies.

Soil conditions

The suitability of the local soil conditions is of paramount importance when planting peonies. Peonies are not particularly fussy about whether the soil is alkaline or acidic (although they will tend to prefer less acidic soils), nor whether the soil is rich in nutrients, sandy or otherwise, but they do require free-draining soil – it's the single most important issue when it comes to soils for peonies. Peonies do not tolerate wet roots and if the soil gets waterlogged then the peony won't thrive and in some cases will deteriorate rapidly. This is largely because peonies have thick, tuberous roots, designed to store food and water and soft-tissue buds below ground ready for next season's growth, both of which will easily rot if held in wet soil. In their native habitats on the sides of rocky mountains and rough, open woodlands, peonies are used to free-draining soil and won't adapt to having wet 'feet'.

Provided it is free-draining, any fertile soil will be acceptable, though with poor soil it may take a little longer for the plant to become fully established to enable plentiful flowering. Peonies do require access to nutrients, as do all plants, so that their roots can store sufficient food to provide the energy needed to enable their extremely rapid growth in early spring. Remember that if you are planting near large shrubs or trees, these will likely absorb much of the nutrients in the surrounding soil to the detriment of the peony, and you may need to provide additional fertiliser and organic matter to the soil.

Peonies grow very well in clay soils, which are generally rich in nutrients, but if the ground is particularly heavy you may need to consider adding some additional organic matter to provide aeration and 'open up' the soil.

Left: Sitting on the planter, bare-root peonies are being sorted for planting in the large peony trial fields.

Time spent preparing the soil in advance is well worth it and well-aerated (that is to say that has an open structure and that is not compacted), fertile and free-draining soil will provide the best possible opportunity for peonies to thrive. Observation is key, though, and it is worth keeping a watchful eye on soil conditions over the decades – from time to time, you may need to top dress with additional organic matter and add additional fertiliser if the soil is poor and not especially well aerated.

Water

Water is, of course, hugely important for the successful growth and development of all plants. With peonies, watering is particularly important in the spring, when the flower buds are developing, and also in late summer/early autumn, when the plant is producing its below-ground growth buds for the following season.

Although well-established peonies will tolerate drought and dry conditions in the summer, they will not generally be creating food and adding to the food storage in their roots, which means that their performance the following season may be impaired and the foliage may die off earlier than would normally be expected. It is best to ensure that peonies do not completely dry out over the summer and are watered regularly. Please do not be tempted to overwater peonies – your peony will not thank you.

Sunlight

Peonies generally perform best in full sunlight. Inadequate sunlight will result in fewer blooms of lesser quality and weaker flower stems and, ultimately, if the level of shade is too great, the loss of flowering completely, followed by the terminal decline of the plant. There are, however, some herbaceous peonies that perform well in shadier positions, and light shade can result in peonies with flowers that have stronger colour and greater fragrance. In order to produce healthy plants with strong stems and plentiful blooms, herbaceous and intersectional peonies require between six and twelve hours of sunlight and woody peonies a little less, perhaps four to six hours each day.

Please do not be tempted to overwater peonies – your peony will not thank you.

Right: New peony shoots seen in early spring as they start to emerge from the ground after winter.

Blooms on peonies that are in direct sunlight will not last quite as long as those with a little afternoon shade and the strength of colour will often fade much more quickly, as you might expect.

How and when to plant

The best time to plant peonies will depend on whether you are planting bare roots or potted peonies. Peonies that have been container grown can be planted at any time of the year, although more care may be required to ensure that the plant has access to sufficient water whilst it becomes established if it is planted in spring or summer. Bare roots must ideally be planted in the autumn, when the plants are fresh and at their most healthy and the plant has the best chance to establish itself before the spring. If the bare roots look a little dry, soak them in a bath of water for about thirty minutes before planting.

Growing peonies is quite easy and straightforward provided they are planted correctly. Being the only major bit of gardening they require, the importance of planting peonies properly cannot be overemphasised. A correctly planted peony will be perfectly happy in its new home for many decades.

The first thing to consider is ground preparation – make sure that the soil is fertile, free-draining and well-aerated and that there is enough space around the proposed planting position. If necessary, dig in some organic matter in advance, which will also aerate the soil.

Dig a planting hole big enough to accommodate the root ball of the plant or the bare root; these can be quite big and chunky, so ensure the roots are not squashed or broken when placed in the planting hole. If the soil conditions are particularly light (for example if the soil is mostly sandy or chalky), dig a slightly deeper planting hole and put 10-15cm or more of organic matter in the bottom before planting the peony. This will not only add to the soil structure but also act as a pad to hold water, preventing water and nutrients from draining away too quickly and giving the peony's roots enough time to absorb them in order to grow. When planting herbaceous and

Left: New buds (or eyes) often look like pink jewels emerging from the soil or woody stems of tree peonies.

intersectional peonies, ensure you place the crown of the root (the top) no more than 2.5-5cm below the soil surface and in the centre of the planting hole. This is extremely important; if planted any deeper, the plant may produce wonderful foliage but is unlikely to ever flower. When planting woody or tree peonies, these should be planted with the crown of the root 10-15cm below the soil surface (this is especially important when planting woody peonies that have been grafted onto a nurse root). Backfill the planting hole with a mixture of soil and organic matter and gently firm the soil around the peony with your hands, trying to avoid compacting the soil too much and/or damaging any of the buds on the roots just below ground (remember, peonies like good aeration, and the purpose of firming the soil is simply to hold the plant in position).

Once planted, it's a good idea to give a light watering and to water gently but regularly if the peony is planted in spring or summer; for peonies planted in the autumn, there is generally sufficient moisture in the soil such that very little watering may be needed, if any. It may also be appropriate to apply a granular slow-release feed before watering in.

Finally, don't forget to label the peony you have just planted. It is useful as a marker to know where herbaceous and intersectional peonies have been planted, as they will die to the ground completely in the autumn/winter. Knowing what variety or cultivar you have planted is essential for future reference, but more importantly this is vital for plant conservation; in years to come (and the peony is likely to be around long after you), proper labelling will assist you and others who are looking to protect our plant heritage.

Whether peonies are in their native habitat or in our gardens, they are fundamental to the future of the genus, providing a rich source of genetic material for hybridisers to create new cultivars and for nature to ensure its survival through adaptation and mutation. Understanding which plants, whether species or cultivated, are commonly found and those that are threatened is critically important to looking after the diversity of plants on our planet.

When planting herbaceous and intersectional peonies, ensure you place the crown of the root (the top) no more than 2.5-5cm below the soil surface.

Top left: Open, free-draining soil with plenty of organic matter is perfect for peonies.

Top right: Make sure your planting hole is wide enough for your peony but not too deep. Planting depth for peonies is really important.

Bottom left: Woody or tree peonies planted with the graft union about 10-15cm below the surface in our production beds.

Bottom right: New shoots emerging in the spring.

There are very many peony species and cultivars that are no longer available through habitat destruction, over extraction from the wild or because newer, stronger cultivars have been produced, or indeed because the cultivar simply fell out of fashion; either way, it is a tragic extinction and permanent loss of our planet's flora and plant heritage. The only hope is that somewhere, someone has a peony in their garden that is a rare species or now unavailable cultivar that is cared for and correctly labelled.

Feeding

Provided soil conditions are reasonable, peonies will not require heavy feeding; in fact, overfeeding can be detrimental to the plant and its abundance of flowering. The addition of manure or other organic matter should ideally be provided before planting a peony and care should be taken when adding further organic matter after planting so as not to create conditions that will facilitate disease around the base of the plant, or indeed over-enrich the soil such that the plant's roots rot. The addition of organic matter after planting could be applied periodically every few years, but I would not necessarily recommend an annual application.

A light feed with a slow-release, well-balanced granular fertiliser once a year in the early spring (just when the plant is shooting) or in the early summer, after the plant has flowered, will usually suffice. When fertilising, remember that the feed should not come into contact with the plant and it will need watering in immediately to avoid burning the foliage or other damage. Generally speaking, liquid feeding during the growing season is to be treated with caution; it will not increase flowering during the season because peonies use the energy stored in their tuberous roots to produce growth buds for the following year and the plant's growth was determined the previous autumn. A well-balanced or low-nitrogen liquid feed in early summer, after the peony has flowered but before the end of the season, is sometimes used perhaps once or twice only to provide a boost to the plant and assist it as it builds its food reserves (this will also keep the plant looking healthy).

Left: Gorgeous peonies against a wall, Spetchley Park Estate & Gardens, Worcestershire.

Plant supports

Some peonies will have either an abundance of gorgeous blooms so large and heavy that the stems cannot hold them up and they will need support. In these cases, staking is recommended. However, species peonies, intersectional peonies and woody peonies are usually able to hold their own blooms without the need for extra staking; it is often the taller herbaceous cultivars that need plant supports and a thoughtful selection can avoid the need for their use.

Proper and regular watering through the growing season and plenty of sunlight will also add strength to the stems of peony plants and reduce the need for plant supports.

The best supports are usually metal cones or ring frames that sit over the plant, which then grows through it. The support must be placed over the plant whilst it is still shooting (if you forget and leave it too late, because peonies grow very quickly in the spring you will find that the plant is already too big. Once in place, the plant growth usually hides the support frame). For exhibition purposes I sometimes stake individual stems holding single blooms, but this is not often necessary in the garden.

Deadheading

Once peonies have flowered, the plant will proceed to produce seedpods and seeds. For some gardeners the dead flower heads are unsightly and these may be removed; cut them off at the top of the flower stem (ideally a junction with a leaf – don't cut the stem back to the ground at this time). In theory, removing the flower heads once they have finished blooming means that the plant does not waste valuable food and energy in producing seedpods and seeds, though I am not certain this makes a significant difference with peonies and certainly in the nursery we do not deadhead the thousands of finished blooms as a matter of course. In fact, the formation of seedpods and seeds is, in my view, very attractive in peonies. The majority of peonies in the garden will be infertile, so the likelihood is that the seed will not be of any use, meaning the only reasons for leaving the bloom to produce seeds and pods would be because you either

Some peonies will have either an abundance of gorgeous blooms so large and heavy that the stems cannot hold them up and they will need support.

Right: Peonies with plant support in the walled garden at Cowdray, West Sussex. © Clive Nichols.

When growing peonies to produce cut flowers, it is sometimes desirable to remove the smaller side buds, leaving the main, central flower.

like the attractive seedpods or simply have better things to do in the garden! Whether you decide to deadhead or not, the important thing is not to cut the plant back to the ground once it has finished flowering, as it is still growing and needs plenty of food and energy to produce growth shoots for the following year.

Disbudding for cut flower blooms

When growing peonies to produce cut flowers, it is sometimes desirable to remove the smaller side buds, leaving the main, central flower bud at the end of the stem (known as disbudding). If removed during the early stages of development whilst the side buds are very small, the plant will redirect the energy from the (now removed) side buds to the single bud on the stem, thus producing a larger, better-quality flower bloom. Disbudding is not essential and unless exhibition-quality cut flowers are required it is something that can be dispensed with. It is certainly not needed for growing peonies in the garden generally; in fact, it is the side buds on the intersectional peonies that provide the unusually long characteristic flowering period because the side buds tend to flower after the main flower has finished. Since this is one of the main attractions of intersectional peonies it seems nonsensical to remove the side buds unless there is very good reason.

End of season care

By late autumn, most peonies, whether herbaceous, intersectional or woody, will have shed their leaves and, in the case of herbaceous and intersectional peonies, died down completely. I tend not to mulch peonies regularly because I find that it can reduce the vitality of the plant and there is the inherent risk that the peony crown becomes buried under the mulch, resulting in a lack of flowering the following year. If you do decide to mulch (perhaps to assist in moisture retention or weed suppression in the border), remember to leave a bare circle of soil around the base of the plant so that the crown isn't covered.

Left: When peonies have finished flowering, their seedheads often have a beauty of their own.

One of the few maintenance tasks the peony gardener must do is to cut back the dead stems and foliage on herbaceous and intersectional peonies. It is important to wait until the plant has completely died down (the leaves and stem will be brown and dead-looking), so please don't be tempted to cut the plant back whilst it is still growing. Cutting back herbaceous and intersectional peonies is very easy: simply using a pair of secateurs, cut the stems back as close to the ground as possible (being careful not to damage any growth buds that may be emerging from or just below the soil). Discard the dead stems and foliage, preferably by burning them, but in any event do not use them in your compost heap. Cutting back the dead foliage will tidy the garden, reduce the possibility of disease and reduce the risk of peony wilt affecting your plants in the spring.

As far as woody or tree peonies are concerned, simply rake up the fallen leaves and dispose of them – this will leave the woody peony framework exposed. The autumn is a good time to prune woody peonies to achieve a more pleasing shape or reduce them in size, but pruning is not mandatory and in most cases the plant will be perfectly happy if it is left as it is. In my experience, woody peonies respond very well to and benefit from good and regular pruning and one shouldn't be afraid of pruning well-established woody peonies hard, as this generally results in lots of new growth the following spring.

Pruning woody peonies

Woody peonies do not need to be towering giants; they respond very well to hard pruning and can be kept neatly in shape in the garden, notwithstanding that some woody peonies tend to flower better on older stems that are two to three years old. The potential sacrifice of some flowers to produce fewer but better-quality flowers and a healthier, more vigorous plant is, I think, well worth it.

It is always a good idea to prune and remove any dead stems. Sometimes stems can become damaged during the winter and removal of these in the spring as close to the ground as possible will keep the plant healthy and tidy looking.

Regular pruning of woody peonies will create a more healthy and vigorous plant.

Right: Cut back herbaceous and intersectional peonies level with the ground in the autumn and dispose of the dead leaves.

A Love Affair with Peonies

Where a peony has one or two old woody stems, pruning the stems back in the autumn by two thirds will be sufficient to encourage new basal growth.

Equally, where a woody stem shows signs of disease, cut the stem back, removing the diseased part and a little extra to ensure that all of the affected area has been taken away. Generally speaking, the plant will recover from such pruning with new growth the following year.

Where a peony has one or two old woody stems, pruning the stems back in the autumn by two thirds will be sufficient to encourage new basal growth. Once the plant has produced new growth, the remaining part of the old stems can be removed. It may take a couple of years for the new growth to reach a size where the old stems can be removed and a little observation and patience will be needed, but the tired, woody peony will be rejuvenated by the pruning treatment.

Where a woody peony has multiple stems densely packed together, it is possible to remove some of them, perhaps every third stem, taking out the older stems first, close to the base, to create space. This will also provide additional light and improve air circulation, both of which are important for the health of the plant, to mitigate the risk of stem disease, improve the overall shape of the plant and maintain its vigour. I would generally prune in this way immediately after the peony has flowered in the spring.

Seasonal care for peonies

Peonies are of interest throughout the year, from the sheer excitement of the new bright red or burgundy shoots unfurling their early foliage at the start of spring to their incredible colour in early autumn. There is the rapid growth of the plant to its full size over just a few weeks in early to late spring, the delicious, fat peony buds holding so much expectant joy, then the gloriously luxurious blooms themselves in early summer, or indeed the splendour of the plant toward the end of the season with wonderful and interesting seedpods. As a low-maintenance plant, there isn't really much to do once the peony has been planted but sit back and enjoy. I cannot think of any other plant that is as interesting and beautiful at all times of the year and at all stages of growth.

Left: Single-flowered varieties are perfect for bees and other pollinators, Hatfield House and Gardens, Hertfordshire.

Though it may seem as if the imminent arrival of winter is killing off your herbaceous and intersectional peonies, bear in mind that the peony's deathly above-ground appearance is its defence against the winter weather and that it is working hard to develop its flower buds for next year. It actually welcomes the cold weather, and as winter fades, as it always does, the peony will emerge victorious in the spring, stronger and with more blooms than in previous years.

Spring

- When the shoots are just emerging from winter, it is a good time to give a well-balanced granular feed.

- If you have a taller herbaceous peony, spring is the time to place a plant support over the peony before it gets too big to manhandle.

- Once the flower buds are starting to form, remember to make sure the plant is watered well so that the buds properly develop. Good watering is important to developing large, healthy flower buds and strong stems to bear the flowers. If you are so inclined, this is the time to start disbudding and removing any unwanted side buds if you are looking to produce a single large bloom for cutting.

- Pruning woody peonies that have multiple densely packed stems once they have flowered can thin out the stems and remove any that are dead or diseased.

Summer

- Once the peony has finished flowering, you may wish to deadhead the plant, removing the finished blooms. Cut just below the bloom, leaving plenty of foliage on the plant (it is still growing and needs the foliage!). Deadheading is not essential in my view – I quite like the developing seedpods, but it's a question of personal choice.

- Whilst peonies will tolerate dry weather, regular watering through the summer will ensure good and strong root growth, enabling bigger and better flowers the following year.

When the shoots are just emerging from winter, it is a good time to give a well-balanced granular feed.

Right: Deadheading peonies. Note the chalky white deposits on the leaves – this is caused by excess calcium in the very hard water at our nursery. It is not detrimental to the plant and will be washed away by rain.

Peonies will still be growing in August and September and preparing for their dormancy in winter, so it's important not to deprive them of their foliage too soon.

Left: Potting in the barn in autumn – five-year-old lifted peonies are potted into commercial pots for sale.

Left: Potting in the barn in autumn – five-year-old lifted peonies are potted into commercial pots for sale.

Pages 78-79: *Paeonia* 'Blushing Princess' in production and growing beautifully in the field.

Autumn

- Don't be tempted to cut back herbaceous peonies that appear to be dying too early. Wait until the foliage has completely died back and then cut the plant back hard to about 2.5cm above the ground, carefully disposing of the foliage. Peonies will still be growing in August and September and preparing for their dormancy in winter, so it's important not to deprive them of their foliage too soon. However, cutting back herbaceous and intersectional peonies in the autumn is worthwhile to improve hygiene generally and reduce the risk of disease in the garden. Whilst herbaceous peonies may look like they are dying above ground, they are in fact working very hard beneath it; the flowering buds for the next year will be developing and growing, so avoid cutting them back until late October/early November. You can do this to about 2.5cm from the ground to help prevent potential disease (such as peony wilt) in the spring. Burn or dispose of the dead foliage to avoid spreading any disease and don't use it in the compost heap.

- Once peonies have entered dormancy for winter, usually in late autumn, they can be divided, lifted and moved in the garden. Autumn is the ideal time to split and move well-established herbaceous peonies, despite the widely held view that peonies don't like being moved. It is best to move your peony in late October.

- Whilst you can plant container-grown peonies in the garden at any time of the year, autumn is the best time to plant bare-root peonies. Remember to buy a good-quality bare-root peony for best results; the mother plants will be lifted from the fields in September/October and split, so if you see bare roots for sale earlier in the year then beware – they may have been sitting in cold storage and potentially be deteriorating. Look for bare roots with at least three to five 'eyes' or buds and remember to plant them with the crown no more than 2.5-5cm below the surface.

- Once woody peonies have lost their leaves, they can be pruned and generally respond well to regular pruning. Woody peonies rarely require pruning, but from time to time it may be necessary to keep well-established plants under control. Autumn is the

Although peonies do not need to be regularly divided for their own benefit, it may be desirable to divide a peony that has got too big for the space available or to create more peony plants for the garden.

ideal time to give woody peonies a light prune – to encourage a better growth habit, cut back the older stems to about 2.5cm or, if in doubt, cut back every third stem; this will produce a bushier plant. Equally, you can lightly trim back to just above the season's new growth to keep your woody peony looking neat and tidy. Pruning in the autumn may mean fewer flowers in the spring, but this is a temporary sacrifice for a stronger, healthier plant in the long term.

• If you have light, sandy soil, consider a second granular feed in late summer or early autumn.

Lifting and moving peonies

As a long-lived plant, peonies will prefer not to be disturbed and moved and this is especially true of woody peonies. However, it is possible to successfully lift, move and divide peonies, provided it is done in late autumn and care is taken not to damage the root system. To avoid any damage to the roots, take as big a clump as possible (ensuring you have at least three to five 'eyes' or buds) and be prepared to re-plant the peony immediately (don't dig it up and leave it for days on end before replanting it). Try not to damage any white, hairy roots, which are very important in waking the peony up in the spring and getting the plant growing. Dig a large enough hole and add some organic matter – remember not to plant your herbaceous or intersectional peony too deep (it will like to feel the cold in the winter, so the crown of the root should not be more than 2.5-5cm below the surface) and to plant woody peonies deep enough (around 10-15cm below the surface). Be patient and allow your peony time to settle into its new position. Given the substantial lifetime of the peony, allowing it a season to settle down is a small price to pay for a long-lived, strong and healthy plant.

Dividing peonies: herbaceous and intersectional peonies

Although peonies do not need to be regularly divided for their own benefit, it may be desirable to divide a peony that has become too big for the space available or to create more peony plants for the garden.

Left: Autumn time on the nursery is very busy with lifting peonies from the fields and potting plants for sale the following spring.

Peonies that have been divided recover well, but note the obvious point that the larger the division of peony the more quickly it will recover and flower again. Lift the peony plant carefully and without damaging the roots (the tuberous roots can easily snap and break and the whitish aerial roots are quite delicate). Carefully brush away as much soil from the roots as possible to enable you to see exactly what you are doing, then, using either a sharp spade or, if the plant is smaller, a knife, cut the root into the desired number of pieces (or 'divisions'), ensuring that each division has at least three to five 'eyes' or buds and a substantial, fat, tuberous root (full of food and energy) to sustain the division once replanted. Cut away any infected or rotten roots and discard. Replant the division in either another part of the garden or in a container. Remember to carefully water the peony the following year as the root system will not be fully developed and avoid overwatering, which may rot the crown of the root.

Dividing peonies: woody or tree

Dividing woody or tree peonies is a little more complex than dividing herbaceous peonies and it is best to do this in mid-autumn when the plant is dormant. It is only really possible to divide multi-stemmed woody peonies so if you have a woody peony with a single stem you will need to prune hard each year to encourage new stems and wait for the plant to become established before it can be divided.

Woody peonies require the above-ground woody stem to remain intact in order to flower. Unlike herbaceous peonies they don't have 'eyes' below ground and the buds appear on the sides of the above-ground stems. Therefore when dividing take extra care to inspect the plant and its roots before you make any cuts; you may find that you can divide the plant with one or two careful cuts. Each division will need a woody stem of around 9-12" (maybe more depending on the size of the roots) supported by as many roots as possible, including fat tuberous roots which contain food for the plant. Remember to plant the divisions immediately and water them well.

The most common disease in peonies is botrytis (also known as peony blight), which, left untended, can be damaging to the plant.

Right: Well-established peony at Hodnet Hall, Shropshire.

Pages 84-85: Part of a long 100-metre peony border at Penshurst Place and Gardens, Kent.

Tough and Versatile

Peonies are incredibly tough and one of the most robust and long-lived herbaceous plants in the garden.

Why are peonies so tough and versatile?

Peonies are incredibly tough and one of the most robust and long-lived herbaceous plants in the garden, despite their beautiful and delicate blooms, and are often seen thriving in neglected gardens.

Peonies are native in various, often surprising, places in the Northern Hemisphere, from Europe and the Mediterranean to the Caucasus and Central Asia and through to China, Japan and parts of the USA. Peonies grow in mountainous areas, woodlands and prairies. With this in mind, it is easy to see how peonies have adapted to a wide range of climatic and environmental temperate conditions, from cold and damp to warm and dry (ideal for cold winters and warm summers). Although native species peonies are not especially common or indeed numerous around the world, their wide distribution is a significant factor in their ability to thrive in the garden. Another major reason for their toughness is that peonies have had plenty of time to evolve and adapt, having been around for more than 100,000 years, making them very good survivors. Part of the survival strategy is clearly a wide global distribution and ability to cope with varying conditions, as well as the fact that the food-storing roots can sustain the peony through a subsequent poor growing season and peony seeds have an extremely

Species Distribution

Left: Peonies as part of a mixed perennial border in early summer, The Manor, Priors Marston, Warwickshire. © Clive Nichols.

Pages 88-89: A close-up of the spectacular 100-metre peony border at Penshurst Place and Gardens, Kent.

hard shell, meaning that the seed remains viable for a longer period of time, ready to germinate when conditions are optimum. Being long-lived plants also creates many opportunities to produce seeds.

Although not ideal for promoting healthy root growth, peonies will tolerate drought in the summer, meaning that once planted they can pretty much be left alone in the garden.

Versatility

For the most part, peonies will do very well in any fertile, free-draining soil in part shade or full sun in a sheltered position in the garden, making them versatile garden plants. Peonies can be grown for cut flower production and for their beauty and fragrance as well as for use in landscape planting schemes, as hedging or as statement plants.

Peonies in full sun or part shade

For more exposed positions in the garden there are more compact peonies that will tolerate this; indeed, intersectional peonies tend to be a good choice because of their sturdy woody peony framework.

Most peonies will prefer full-sun positions in the garden in order to maximise flower production. There are some that are quite happy in partial shade (although not heavy shade) and I find that these peonies hold their fragrance better (generally because it is not evaporated so quickly by the heat of the day) and are often very delicate and beautiful, *Paeonia lactiflora* 'White Wings' or *Paeonia anomla* subsp. *veitchii* AGM, for example. Woody peonies will often tolerate partial shade, provided that they get four or more hours of sunlight each day.

Peonies as border plants

Peonies can grow to become substantial woody shrubs, 1.2-1.5m tall and even some of the herbaceous peonies can reach over 1m, making them ideal plants when placed

Peonies will do very well in any fertile, free-draining soil in part shade or full sun in a sheltered position in the garden, making them versatile garden plants.

Above: Herbaceous peonies in part shade at Birtsmorton Court, Worcestershire.
© Clive Nichols.

Page 92: Part-shade herbaceous border at the walled garden at Cowdray, West Sussex.
© Clive Nichols.

Page 93: Full-sun herbaceous border at Birtsmorton Court, Worcestershire.
© Clive Nichols.

towards the back of a border. The vast majority of peonies grow to around 90cm, but there are some shorter cultivars that are perfect in the middle of the border, such as *Paeonia lactiflora* 'Gay Paree' AGM, and some that are better suited to the front of the border, such as *Paeonia officinalis* 'Anemoniflora Rosea' AGM.

Intersectional peonies are excellent for the centre or back of borders, growing to around 90cm tall and with a solid, compact habit, which can be very dominant in a smaller or narrow border but perfect in a traditional herbaceous border.

Peonies as landscape plants

For mass planting, the reliable *Paeonia lactiflora* 'Krinkled White', which often does not need staking, makes a good hedge, with lots of single white flowers with crinkled petals on mid-green foliage. However, if grown a little more closely together, many peonies will provide each other with support, negating the need for plant supports entirely. Equally, peonies work very well as centrepieces or statements in the garden and can easily provide a focal point in the summer.

Pests and diseases

Peonies are pretty tough garden plants and rarely suffer significant damage from pests and disease. None of the wildlife on our nursery troubles peonies (although the alpacas did escape once and managed to eat the top growth on some of them; this didn't cause any long-term harm, but I was worried until I saw the plants re-shooting the following spring!). Aphids, slugs, snails, rabbits and deer tend to avoid peonies. From time to time I am asked about ants, but generally speaking the ants are interested in the sweet sap on the flower buds and they don't cause any damage to the plant, leaving entirely once the flowers have opened.

Disease in peonies is usually a result of poor growing conditions placing the plant under stress, prolonged periods of wet, humid weather, for example, and a lack of airflow around the plant or pools of water on the soil around the crown. Equally, stress induced as a result of too little water can make the plant more susceptible to disease, making it important to ensure that growing conditions are carefully considered at the outset when planting and are monitored over the years as the plant, and the garden around it, grow.

The most common disease in peonies is botrytis (also known as peony blight), which, left untended, can be damaging to the plant. It is relatively easy to identify, though, and usually quick action to remove the infected stems or parts of the plant will ensure that there will be no long-term damage. Often, parts of the peony, typically

Peonies are pretty tough garden plants and rarely suffer significant damage from pests and disease.

Top left: Ants on peony buds are not generally a problem and should be left undisturbed.

Top right: Peony blight is not normally detrimental to the long-term viability of mature peonies provided it is cut out and destroyed immediately.

Below: Peonies can be used to make a beautiful and fragrant border hedge.

Peony blight is more prevalent in wet weather, especially in the spring, and good airflow around the plant is very important.

affecting stems, buds and leaves, will become a dark brown colour before wilting and then dying. Later in the season the plant may have brown spots on the leaves, which again is botrytis. There are chemical controls that can be used, but I find that decisive action to cut out and destroy any infected material is sufficient to ensure that there is no lasting detrimental effect on the peony. It is important to know that if the infected plant material (whilst still attached to the plant or otherwise) comes into contact with the leaves of another peony, that peony will then become infected, so dispose of any infected material by burning it (don't put it on the compost heap) and disinfect your secateurs afterwards.

It's worth checking the plant regularly after you have removed any infected material just to be sure that you have taken all affected parts have been removed. Peony blight is more prevalent in wet weather, especially in the spring, and good airflow around the plant is very important. Good hygiene in the garden will help too, and cutting back and disposing of dead foliage in the autumn and disposing of it aids greatly in reducing the risk of disease.

Peonies can also suffer from viruses and whilst the plant may not necessarily die immediately, it will lack vigour and will gradually decline. In most instances, the only solution is to dig up the plant and burn it, making sure that your tools have been disinfected properly to reduce the risk of further transmission.

Frost

Although peonies are hardy, mostly down to temperatures of -20°C, new growth in the spring can be vulnerable and flower buds can be affected by late frosts. The plant generally will not suffer too much and usually bounce back the following spring showing no signs of the previous year's trials and tribulations, but the loss of flower buds is always a severe disappointment, especially when it occurs at around the time you are expecting to see blooms begin to open.

Left: On the Primrose Hall Peonies nursery we grow peonies in tunnels as well as outside. Here a mixture of peony varieties, including *Paconia* 'Rcd Charm' AGM, as seen in tunnel two.

Pages 98-99: *Paeonia* 'Scarlet O'Hara' AGM.

A Riot of Colour

With the exception of blue and black, peonies bloom in all shades of colour, from pure white to deep burgundy and purple hues. Some peony flowers are bicoloured and some are even tricoloured for added interest.

Flower blooms and colour selection

Peonies come in a bewildering range of colours that can create peace and tranquillity, dreamy romance or vibrant drama in the garden. The colour combinations are immense and with careful companion planting peonies can create and hold together distinct theatrical moods, although caution should be exercised, as they can easily become dominant in a border. With the exception of blue and black, peonies bloom in all shades of colour, from pure white to deep burgundy and purple hues. Some peony flowers are bicoloured and some are even tricoloured for added interest.

One of the most pleasing and interesting characteristics of some peonies is that their blooms change colour as they mature. The most clear example of this is perhaps *Paeonia* 'Coral Sunset' AGM, which initially opens as a deep, bright pink before slowly fading to a beautiful coral colour, then pale lemon shades before finishing a dirty cream (often with some petals brown by the end). The transition from pink to cream usually takes about six or seven days, and with many blooms on one or more plants, each at a different colour stage, the effect can be quite spectacular, making the 'Coral Sunset' name quite appropriate.

It is also worth pointing out that the colour of a particular peony bloom can vary as a result of local environmental conditions, such as soil conditions and levels of sunlight, but also because of the age of the bloom (as discussed above), which sometimes makes describing peony flower colours very difficult. For example, peonies grown on heavier soils and clay can often have stronger flower colours than the same plants grown on lighter, sandier soils and blooms that open on cooler, more overcast days will often fade in colour less quickly.

Left: Fabulous autumn foliage on an intersectional peony.

Autumn colour from peonies

There are lots of jobs to keep the gardener busy in autumn: raking leaves, collecting seed, dividing plants and generally tidying up. For the peony gardener, there is perhaps a little less to do and more time to enjoy the pleasures of autumn, reflecting on the gardening triumphs of the summer. For me, the highlight of the summer is unquestionably during the relatively short flowering window (late April to June), when peonies are in full, majestic flower, but as the summer comes to an end, the foliage of peonies, and especially intersectional peonies, unfailingly brings unexpected pleasure and interest.

Herbaceous peonies that die down completely in the winter have the strongest autumnal colour, with the intersectional varieties (such as *Paeonia* 'Morning Lilac' AGM) providing a strong, dignified show of orange, red, green and purple foliage whilst the remainder of the garden is in decline. Some of the earlier flowering varieties, such as *Paeonia x festiva* 'Rubra Plena' AGM or *Paeonia* 'Coral Charm' AGM, may start to change colour and die off whilst the remainder of the garden is in full summer swing in early August, but others, such as *Paeonia lactiflora* 'Catharine Fontijn', *Paeonia lactiflora* 'Doreen' AGM or *Paeonia lactiflora* 'Peter Brand', will provide you with incredible bright pink and red foliage in the autumn. Woody peonies (for example, *Paeonia x lemoinei* 'High Noon' AGM) can be equally impressive before they too lose their large, divided leaves, leaving their woody stems nobly standing proud in the flower beds. Even as the peony dies down for the winter, it does so gracefully and with panache, reminding us of its status as a pre-eminent garden plant and of its flowering glory earlier in the summer.

As the summer comes to an end, the foliage of peonies, and especially intersectional peonies, unfailingly brings unexpected pleasure and interest.

Right: Autumn foliage on intersectional peonies ranges from golden brown to oranges and reds.

The changing colours of peonies

Facing page: The colour fade on *Paeonia* 'Coral Charm' AGM seen transitioning from bright coral, peach, to lemon yellow and then cream. Page 107: *Paeonia* 'Old Faithful' is an excellent example of a peony flower changing colour from ruby red to an antique rose pink fade.

1. Opens bright pink.

2. Colour softens to pale pink.

3. Colour changes to salmon.

4. Colour fades to coral.

5. Bloom lightens to pale peach.

6. Finally fades to pale yellow and cream.

Peonies by Colour

Here is a non-exhaustive list, a few of my favourites.

Red

America

Big Ben

Blaze AGM

Christmas Velvet

Diana Parks

Henry Bockstoce

Inspecteur Lavergne

Lorelei

Miss Mary

Nippon Beauty

Old Faithful

Paul M. Wild

Red Charm AGM

Red Grace

Scarlet Heaven

Sonoma Velvet

Sword Dance AGM

Victoire de la Marne

Lilac and Purple

First Arrival AGM

Morning Lilac AGM

Norwegian Blush

Pastel Splendor

Purple Spider

Sonoma Amethyst

Pink

Albert Crousse

Alexander Fleming

Alice Harding

Angel Cheeks

Best Man

Birthday

Blushing Princess

Bouquet Perfect AGM

Bowl of Beauty

Dinner Plate

Edulis Superba

Helen Hayes

Hillary

Madame Calot

Monsieur Jules Elie AGM

My Love

Pillow Talk

Pink Parfait

Seashell

Show Girl

The Fawn AGM

Yankee Doodle Dandy

Bi-Colour

Candy Stripe

Cora Louise AGM

Lollipop

Coral and Orange

Apricot Queen

Coral Charm AGM

Coral Magic

Coral Supreme

Kopper Kettle

Salmon Chiffon

Salmon Dream

Soft Salmon Saucer

Yellow

Bartzella AGM

Border Charm

Claire de Lune AGM

Garden Treasure

Going Bananas

mlokosewitschii AGM

Sequestered Sunshine

Sonoma Halo

Starlight

Yellow Crown

White and Cream

Avalanche

Baroness Schroeder

Boule de Neige

Bowl of Cream

Bridal Gown

Duchesse de Nemours AGM

Elsa Sass

Festiva Maxima AGM

Immaculee AGM

Jan van Leeuwen AGM

Madame Claude Tain

Mother's Choice

Shirley Temple AGM

Top Brass

White Emperor

White Frost AGM

White, Cream and Blush

Paeonia lactiflora 'White Wings'

Paeonia emodi AGM

Paeonia 'White Emperor'

Paeonia suffruticosa 'Fuso Tsukasa'

Paeonia 'Love Affair'

Paeonia 'Queen of Hearts'

Paeonia lactiflora 'Honey Gold'

Paeonia lactiflora 'Charles White'

Paeonia x festiva 'Alba Plena'

Paeonia lactiflora 'Carl G Klehm'

Paeonia lactiflora 'Duchesse de Nemours' AGM

Paeonia lactiflora 'Shirley Temple' AGM

Paeonia lactiflora 'Festiva Maxima' AGM

Paeonia lactiflora 'Florence Nicholls' AGM

Paeonia lactiflora 'Immaculee'

Paeonia lactiflora 'Fringed Ivory'

Paeonia lactiflora 'Miss America'

Paeonia lactiflora 'Top Brass'

Yellow

Paeonia 'Garden Treasure'

Paeonia 'Lemon Chiffon' AGM

Paeonia 'Claire de Lune' AGM

Paeonia x lemoinei 'High Noon' AGM

Paeonia 'Bartzella' AGM

Paeonia 'Sonoma Yedo'

Paeonia suffruticosa 'Okan'

Paeonia 'Joanna Marlene'

Paeonia 'Sonoma Sun'

Paeonia lactiflora 'Green Lotus'

Coral and Orange

Paeonia 'Apricot Queen'

Paeonia 'Coral Charm' AGM

Paeonia 'Coral Sunset' AGM

Paeonia 'Singing in the Rain'

Paeonia 'Sonoma Welcome'

Paeonia 'Orange Victory'

Paeonia 'Court Jester'

Paeonia 'Coral Scout'

Paeonia 'Sonoma Floozy'

Paeonia 'Fantasia'

Paeonia lactiflora 'Reine Hortense'

Paeonia 'Madame Calot'

Paeonia lactiflora 'Noemie Demay' AGM

Paeonia lactiflora 'Catharina Fontijn'

Paeonia suffruticosa 'Shimano Fuji'

Paeonia lactiflora 'Pink Parfait'

Paeonia lactiflora 'Eden's Perfume'

Paeonia lactiflora 'Do Tell'

Pink

Paeonia lactiflora 'Lady Anna'

Paeonia lactiflora 'The Fawn' AGM

Paeonia lactiflora 'Sarah Bernhardt' AGM

Paeonia suffruticosa 'Yachiyo-tsubaki'

Paeonia lactiflora 'Nymphe'

Paeonia lactiflora 'Candy Stripe'

Paeonia 'Julia Rose'

Paeonia lactiflora 'Edulis Superba'

Paeonia 'Sonoma Blessing'

Paeonia veitchii var. *woodwardii* AGM

Paeonia lactiflora 'Doreen' AGM

Paeonia lactiflora 'Wladyslawa' AGM

Paeonia 'Sonoma Amethyst'

Paeonia 'Birthday'

Paeonia lactiflora 'Neon'

Paeonia 'First Arrival' AGM

Paeonia 'Watermelon Wine' AGM

Paeonia 'Renato'

Pink

Paeonia 'Old Rose Dandy'

Paeonia 'Etched Salmon'

Paeonia 'Magical Mystery Tour'

Paeonia 'Hillary'

Paeonia lactiflora 'Bouquet Perfect' AGM

Paeonia suffruticosa 'Sedai'

Paeonia 'Pastel Splendor'

Paeonia lactiflora 'Bowl of Beauty'

Paeonia lactiflora 'Alexander Fleming'

Paeonia officinalis 'Anemoniflora Rosea' AGM

Paeonia 'Cuckoo's Nest'

Paeonia 'Walter Mains'

Paeonia suffruticosa 'Kokuryu-nishiki'

Paeonia mollis

Paeonia lactiflora 'Best Man'

Paeonia lactiflora 'Sebastien Maas'

Paeonia lactiflora 'Nice Gal'

Paeonia 'Kansas'

Dark Pink, Red, Crimson and Purple

Paeonia suffruticosa 'Shimazukurenai'

Paeonia lactiflora 'Peter Brand'

Paeonia 'Command Performance'

Paeonia 'Buckeye Belle'

Paeonia 'Sonoma Ruby Velvet'

Paeonia 'Scarlet Heaven'

Paeonia x festiva 'Rubra Plena' AGM

Paeonia 'Scarlet O'Hara' AGM

Paeonia peregrina 'Otto Froebel'

Paeonia 'Red Charm' AGM

Paeonia 'Joyce Ellen'

Paeonia lactiflora 'Miss Mary'

Paeonia 'Flame'

Paeonia 'Eliza Lundy' AGM

Paeonia lactiflora 'Philippe Rivoire'

Paeonia 'America'

Paeonia lactiflora 'Inspecteur Lavergne'

Paeonia 'Morning Lilac' AGM

Gorgeous peonies at Penshurst Place
and Gardens, Kent.

Peonies as Cut Flowers

Peonies are undoubtedly one of the showiest plants, with big, blousy, majestic blooms in glorious colours and shapes that are the definitive icon of luxury in the garden or home.

Strong-stemmed and tall, with a vase life of seven to ten days, peonies make excellent cut flowers, the perfect gift to celebrate special occasions and mark a moment in time, or, indeed, just to brighten your living space. Cutting peonies that you have grown is incredibly satisfying, bringing them with you to further experience, admire and enjoy.

Peonies are grown for commercial cut flower production around the world, from Holland, France and the UK to Israel, New Zealand, the USA and Canada, making them potentially available for a large part of the year.

Cut flower peony production is perhaps more costly than some other cut flower crops due to the time it takes for the plants to sufficiently mature and, of course, because peonies flower only once in a season, providing a single crop. Peonies are rarely grown with heat in glasshouses and as a result are mostly at the mercy of the weather in the field. There is also a risk that when large numbers of peonies are picked in bud, a percentage may refuse to open, meaning that florists and flower arrangers often need to overorder to ensure they have sufficient supply for their designs and creations, all of which potentially increases the end price to the consumer. For most of us, however, peonies are in most abundant supply in early summer from local peony growers, with a consequently more affordable price.

Well-established and mature plants will provide very many blooms for cut flowers and their season can be extended with careful selection to ensure you have both early flowering and late flowering peonies. It may take three or four years after planting before a peony plant produces a good number of flower blooms of suitable quality for cutting, so a little patience may be required.

Left: *Paenoia* 'Coral Charm' AGM makes a wonderful cut flower.

When choosing peonies for cut flowers in the garden, it is worth considering the more fragrant and perfumed varieties. Many of the single-flowered examples are not as scented, so focus instead on the semi-doubles and doubles, which often hold their blooms for longer too.

When picking your peonies as cut flowers, do so when they are in soft bud and not in open flower (a soft bud feels like a marshmallow when gently squeezed between your fingers). If the bud is hard, it is not yet ready and will be unlikely to open properly or at all. If picked in bud, peonies can easily be kept in cold storage for four to six weeks, but blooms that have been held in cold storage usually tend not to last as well in the vase and shatter more quickly.

There is, in my experience, very limited scope to manipulate growing conditions to either force early flowering or delay flowering, which we must do from time to time to meet our exhibition schedule, and it is always stressful. Forcing peonies to flower is not easy and always a little precarious. Growing them under cover (we use polytunnels) will usually bring flowering forward a week or two without the assistance of artificial heat, while holding back peonies to delay flowering is perhaps more difficult, as the blooms often do not last as well (a potential problem if we are exhibiting at a five- or six-day flower show). We often try to 'trick' the plant by delaying its overall development and growth – once the bud has formed, as mentioned, there is little opportunity to hold it back with good results. We may therefore use cold storage to convince the plant it is still winter and to persuade it to remain dormant a little longer than it might usually be, thus delaying its growth and bud production; again, we must be careful – left too late in the season, the buds simply will not develop properly. The window for manipulation is limited if you want to have good-quality blooms. Fresh is always best, however, and with the right selection of peony plants in the garden you will have a plentiful supply of blooms each year.

When picking your peonies as cut flowers, do so when they are in soft bud and not in open flower

Right: Model pictured on our Primrose Hall Peonies nursey holding a voluptuous bunch of *Paeonia lactiflora* 'Alexander Fleming', a wonderfully scented double peony which makes a great cut flower.

For the best cut flower blooms, it is best to remove smaller side buds from the plant as early as possible, leaving a single, central bud on each stem as the focus of the plant's energies. Disbudding need not take too long (provided you only have a few plants to deal with) and will result in bigger and better blooms, perfect for cutting and exhibiting.

As soon as you have cut the peonies (usually with a 50-60cm stem), remove the lower foliage and place the cut stems immediately into a bucket of warm water for about thirty minutes. If you are concerned about ants (and ants love the sweet, sticky sap), just rinse the cut flower buds in warm water before you take them into the house. Once inside, place the peonies in a vase with water and some cut flower food; the peonies will open fully in the vase within two to three days and will generally last seven to ten days. To extend the vase life, I would recommend refreshing the water and recutting the bottom of the stems every three days or so and placing them out of direct sunlight and away from heat sources, such as radiators.

Top tips for growing peonies for cut flowers

1. Look at the flowering times of the peonies. With careful selection you can have cut flowers from the end of April until the end of June.
2. Plant your peony in a sunny, sheltered position in the garden. Any fertile soil will do, but it must be free draining.
3. Plant peonies for cut flower production closer together, perhaps 12-18" apart, to provide mutual support and reduce the need for plant supports.
4. In early spring, when the buds are forming, remove any side buds, leaving a single bloom on each stem to ensure a larger, more impressive bloom.
5. Remember to water your peony in the spring, when the buds are developing. This will prevent them dying off and ensure the plant has nice, straight stems.
6. Feed your peony once a year with a general, well-balanced feed.

Left: Sumptuous pink peonies never get boring. These beauties can be seen at Hatfield House and Gardens, Hertfordshire.

Peonies for Cut Flowers

Right: Peonies are cut flowers adored by florists for the sheer opulence and size in arrangements. There are many varieties of peonies that are perfect for use as cut flowers.

Here is a non-exhaustive list, a few of my favourites.

Red

Command Performance

Flame

Henry Bockstoce

Karl Rosenfield

Old Faithful

Red Charm AGM

Pink

Alertie

Alexander Fleming

Angel Cheeks

Bouchela

Catharina Fontijn

Jadwiga

Kansas

Lady Alexandra Duff

Monsieur Jules Elie

Noemie Demay AGM

Sarah Bernhardt AGM

Sebastian Maas

Coral

Coral Charm AGM

Coral Sunset AGM

Pink Hawaiian Coral

Yellow

Bartzella AGM

White

Albert Crousse

Baroness Schroeder

Bowl of Cream

Duchesse de Nemours AGM

Festiva Maxima AGM

Honey Gold

Mother's Choice

Peonies are a symbol of love and romance.
Pictured is *Paeonia* 'Red Charm' AGM.

We are proud to supply peonies to many award-winning gardens at flower shows. Pictured is *Paeonia lactiflora* 'Lady Anna' on the Mothers for Mothers Garden 'This Too Shall Pass' exhibit at RHS Chelsea Flower Show 2022, designed by Pollyanna Wilkinson, winner of the 2022 RHS People's Choice Award in the Sanctuary Garden category.

Fabulous Peony Flowers

Development in peonies is highly dependent on temperature, and an extended period of cold, damp, overcast weather in the early spring can easily delay flowering by three to four weeks.

Peony flowers are simply exquisite. Decadent and luxurious, the blooms borne by the peony plant are perhaps one of the most important and show-stopping characteristics of these glorious garden plants.

Whilst species peonies often have very simple (yet incredibly magnificent) flowers, with perhaps only five petals, natural mutations and centuries of breeding practice to enhance desirable features have resulted in many of the different peony flowers and forms that we have today, some with many petals and some with a flower within a flower, making huge masses of petals and very attractive double blooms.

Development in peonies is highly dependent on temperature, and an extended period of cold, damp, overcast weather in the early spring can easily delay flowering by three to four weeks, as the flower bud stops developing completely when the weather is cold. In some instances this leads to a very disappointing season, where buds simply fail to develop and die off entirely. Thankfully, this is not a common occurrence, but the susceptibility to temperature of peonies does enable us to manipulate growing conditions and delay flowering for exhibitions to some degree.

The maturity of peony plants can lead to variations in flower shape and colour. Whilst the plant is young, the flower may not only produce different colour flowers but also the characteristic flower type of a particular cultivar does not crystallise and settle until it reaches around five years old. This means that, with new cultivars especially, it is important to observe a plant for a couple of years before being certain of its flower form and colour.

Left: *Paeonia suffruticosa* 'Yachiyo-tsubaki' has magnificent rose-pink semi-double flowers with sumptuous dark foliage.

Flower forms/types

Due to their fertility and variability there are many different forms of peony flowers, and this is one of the reasons why they are so delightful. Different standards are used when describing peony flower types and the American Peony Society officially recognises six different flower forms: single, Japanese, anemone, semi-double, full double and bomb. This classification only really relates to herbaceous peonies (for woody peonies are sometimes described slightly differently) but is useful when describing the flowers. The flower form of a peony may change and develop through the recognised different forms from time to time, usually when the plant is young or in response to temperature and weather, the point in time in the season or because of other temporary cultural conditions. The flower form may also affect the longevity of the bloom, with double flowers tending to last longer than single or bomb type flowers before shattering (although, of course, pollinators much prefer the single type flowers because of the ease of access to the pollen).

Parts of the peony flower

Peony flowers obviously differ, but in the main the bud, containing the petals, stamens and carpels, is held by green sepals. The outer petals of the flower are known as guard petals and often form part of the showy bloom when it is fully open. The stamens are comprised of the filament (the stem part) and the anthers (capsules containing pollen found at the end of the filament). The carpels are found in the centre of the flower (which holds the ovaries that form seedpods) and can be creamy-white, green, or sometimes dark red or purple in colour. The tip of the carpel, the stigma, has a receptive, sticky surface perfect for collecting pollen for fertilisation.

Extending the flowering season

Although individual plants may flower for only ten to fourteen days in the season, this does make flowering something of an event to be celebrated, and with careful selection peonies can flower from late April until early July (depending on local conditions and weather patterns).

The outer petals of the flower are known as guard petals and often form part of the showy bloom when it is fully open.

Right: *Paeonia officinalis* 'Anemoniflora Rosea' AGM, a compact variety, has vibrant bright pink flowers with a splash of gold.

Peony Season in the UK

Here are small selection of my favourites:

Early

America

Carol

Claire de Lune AGM

daurica subsp. *mlokosewitschii* AGM

Moonrise

Scarlet O'Hara AGM

Starlight

tenuifolia

x *festiva* 'Alba'

x *festiva* 'Rubra Plena'

Mid

Antwerpen

Bouquet Perfect AGM

Bridal Shower

Candy Stripe

Green Lotus

Lemon Dream

Lovely Rose

Miss Mary

Pink Ardour

Prairie Charm

Late

Brother Chuck

Couronne D'Or

Elsa Sass

Jadwiga

Madame Claude Tain

Myrtle Gentry

Pink Parfait

President Wilson

Shirley Temple AGM

Solange

Top left: *Paeonia* 'Early Windflower', an early season flowering peony.

Top right: *Paeonia anomala* subsp. *veitchii* AGM, an early to mid-season flowering peony.

Bottom left: *Paeonia lactiflora* 'Catharina Fontijn', a mid-season flowering peony.

Bottom right: *Paeonia lactiflora* 'Paul M. Wild', a late season flowering peony.

Early · Early/Mid · Mid · Mid/Late · Late

Paeonia 'Early Windflower' · *Paeonia* 'Bowl of Beauty' · *Paeonia* 'Jadwiga' · *Paeonia* 'Old Faithful'

April · May · June · July

In early to mid-May, the peony season is well underway and the intersectional peonies begin to flower.

Paeonia 'Claire de Lune' AGM is a hybrid, flowering in late April (early season) with masses of clear, pale yellow flowers, a beautiful fragrance and a bluish tinge to the foliage. It has quite a lax habit and does not generally need staking (making it a more reliable and interesting alternative to *Paeonia daurica* subsp. *mlokosewitschii* AGM, which can be variable in its flowering). For a compact, tough, early flowering peony you might also consider *Paeonia tenuifolia* 'Rubra Plena'. This peony has very fine fern-like foliage, grows to about 60cm and has brilliant red, highly scented flowers. On the subject of foliage, don't forget the ground cover provided by *Paeonia emodi* AGM and its smaller, white, downward-facing flowers on large, divided, pale green foliage. Towards the end of April we also see woody peonies coming into flower, providing height and structure in addition to very large, stunning flowers in all colours. *Paeonia suffruticosa* 'Kokuryu-nishiki' is a favourite woody peony of mine because it has extraordinary deep purple flowers with creamy white stripes. Also consider *Paeonia suffruticosa* 'Yachiyo-tsubaki', a stunning and compact woody peony with gorgeous clear pink semi-double flowers, dark grey/green foliage and pink new-season growth on the stem.

In early May the coral herbaceous peonies are in flower (*Paeonia* 'Coral Sunset' AGM, 'Coral Charm' AGM and 'Coral Supreme'), together with favourites such as *Paeonia lactiflora* 'Duchesse de Nemours' AGM, with its creamy white, fully double, highly fragrant flowers on dark green, glossy leaves. In early to mid-May, the peony season is well underway and the intersectional peonies begin to flower. Intersectional peonies will often flower for longer than a woody peony, for three to four weeks or more. There are many mid-season flowering peonies that will flower into June, and some varieties, *Paeonia lactiflora* 'Victoire de la Marne' or *Paeonia lactiflora* 'Solange', for example, will flower at the end of June and into July.

Top left: *Paeonia tenuifolia* 'Rubra Plena'.
Top right: *Paeonia* 'Clare de Lune' AGM.
Bottom left: *Paeonia* 'Coral Sunset' AGM.
Bottom right: *Paeonia* 'Cuckoo's Nest'.

Japanese

These flowers are similar to single flowers, with an open, flat saucer shape, but in their centre, in place of stamens bearing pollen, they have staminodes (stamens that have not developed in the normal way), which are thicker, broader and do not carry as much pollen, although this is still often feasible enough.

Anemone

In anemone type flowers, the shape is similar to the Japanese but the stamens are no longer recognisable, replaced with small, thin petals known as petalodes. The petalodes can be the same colour as the guard petals or a pale yellow or cream shade.

Bomb

Bomb type flowers are a development of the anemone type flower where the petalodes in the centre become larger and more visible, often the colour of the guard petals and the texture of petals (known as inner petals). The inner petals, the centre of the flower, become quite large and raised, forming a mound or ball shape, and as a result the flower can be quite heavy.

Semi-double

Semi-double flowers are very common and have multiple layers of petals, making the flower more substantial. The flower may have some limited stamens that have developed into inner petals or simply a cluster of stamens in the centre of the fully opened flower.

Full Double

Double peony flowers contain a flower within a flower, and this is how the fully double peonies achieve a large, puffball flower form. Stamens are essentially replaced with petals (although sometimes some stamens are just about visible), such that there is a large number of similar-sized petals overall. It isn't just the vast number of petals that make a double peony form – it is technically the flower within a flower structure.

Single

Single flower types usually have one or two rounds of petals with lots of golden stamens bearing pollen and functioning carpels. The flower shape is generally open and flat, similar to a saucer shape.

> *If a plant has previously flowered reliably then it is clearly of sufficient maturity. The most likely cause of a decline in flowering is either a lack of sunlight or the crown of the plant having been buried.*

Reasons why a peony may not flower

There are few reasons why a peony may not flower and in my view it really boils down to the basics with peonies: soil condition, planting depth, plant maturity and sunlight.

1 Peony has flowered previously but no longer flowers well or at all

If a plant has previously flowered reliably then it is clearly of sufficient maturity. The most likely cause of a decline in flowering is either a lack of sunlight or the crown of the plant having been buried. Lack of sunlight is potentially a bigger issue than many think, and as a long-lived plant the peony often battles on even though the plants, shrubs and trees around it become overgrown, unkempt or just much bigger over time. Equally, diligent gardeners often mulch their borders and in the process cover the crown of the herbaceous or intersectional peony, burying it more than 2.5-5cm below the surface and thus sending the plant into dormancy and, ultimately, terminal decline. Remember, therefore, that peonies are low maintenance, and if you are going to mulch your borders, leave a clear area around the base of your herbaceous peonies.

2 Peony has never flowered

If your peony has never flowered, asking the following questions will generally resolve most flowering issues:

- **Is the plant mature enough, or is it juvenile?** Juvenile plants, less than five years old or so, will often flower intermittently and do not flower reliably until the plant is at least five years old. For woody peonies reliable flowering can take a little longer, sometimes seven to eight years.

Left: Peonies flowering in abundance in mid summer. © Clive Nichols.

- **Is the peony planted too deep (if it is a herbaceous or intersectional peony)?** Remember that the crown of the peony should not be planted more than 2.5-5cm below the surface. If it is too deep, you may have wonderful foliage for some years, but the peony will simply refuse to flower. Planting peonies too deep is the most likely cause of non-flowering in peonies in my experience.

- **Is the peony getting sufficient sunlight?** More established plants that are flowering well may require a little less sunlight, but in the main, peonies require plenty of sunlight to produce an abundance of flowers.

- **Does the peony look unhappy?** Does it have a few weak stems and fails to produce a nice healthy-looking plant? If so, the soil conditions are likely the cause and usually it is because of waterlogging or at least very wet ground during the winter, which is damaging the underground buds, or eyes, on the roots, thus preventing plentiful stems and shoots in the spring.

3 Peony buds go brown and die

This problem is particularly depressing because having waited for so long for buds to appear, they then fail to materialise into the gorgeous blooms we are expecting. Usually, when peonies produce small, brown buds that then simply die off it is because of either a lack of water in the spring when the bud is developing, immaturity of the plant, a lack of nutrients or indeed a lack of sunlight at the crucial time which then prevents the bud from further development (for example if the peony is planted too close to larger, perennial plants that are putting on significant growth in the early spring or if the peony is planted under

Remember that the crown of the peony should not be planted more than 2.5-5cm below the surface.

Top left: Healthy buds developing in spring on *Paeonia* 'Lemon Chiffon' AGM.

Left middle: Underdeveloped peony buds can be caused by various environmental factors.

Left bottom: Peony buds can be aborted because of botrytis, often following a period of wet weather.

Above: Well-established peonies at Spetchley Park Estate & Gardens, Worcestershire.

Pages 148-149: Mixed peony border including foxgloves seen at Wrest Park, Bedfordshire.

a deciduous tree that then comes into leaf when the peony buds are growing). Late, heavy frosts can sometimes cause buds to die off and go brown although in the UK this is rarely a major problem; a more common issue in recent years has been sustained cold temperatures in the spring which stops buds from developing. Planting your peony in full or part sun, in fertile, free-draining soil and ensuring it has access to sufficient water in the spring should address all of these potential causes of bud failure. Sometimes when a bud has developed it turns brown, becomes soft and papery and does not open. This can be caused by botrytis, which is common and more prevalent during lengthy periods of damp or wet weather in the spring. Once the bud has reached this stage it will not open and should be removed from the plant and destroyed. Invariably, if swift action is taken, the plant will not suffer the following year. Good hygiene practices, such as cutting the plant back to the ground in the autumn and removing the dead material and ensuring there is good airflow around the peony plant, will help to reduce the likelihood of botrytis.

The Perfume of Peonies

People are often surprised to learn that peonies can be scented, which is odd, because there are so many peonies that are fragrant.

Early summer in the garden just isn't the same without the spectacle of peonies flaunting masses of striking flowers and exerting a commanding presence in the flower border. Stunning though the blooms are, however, peonies offer more, overwhelming your senses and romancing you with their fragrance, which can be captivating and incredible.

People are often surprised to learn that peonies can be scented, which is odd, because there are so many peonies that are fragrant. Perhaps it is because the old-fashioned double red peony we are familiar with has little or no fragrance (*Paeonia x festiva* 'Rubra Plena' AGM – none the less a cracking plant and recipient of the Award of Garden Merit by the Royal Horticultural Society). It's also fair to say that the single peonies rarely possess a strong scent, so look for the double and semi-double peonies for the best perfumes. Admittedly some peonies are more delicately scented than others, but the more heavily scented peonies are quite something, with plenty of them to choose from. The fragrance can be musky, sweet or rose-like, and some have a citrus or spicy scent. *Paeonia lactiflora* 'Festiva Maxima' AGM is heavily scented with a sweet perfume and *Paeonia lactiflora* 'Duchesse de Nemours' AGM is a sumptuous white with a pale cream ruffled centre and a sweet, fresh, intoxicating scent. Another great perfumed peony is *Paeonia* 'Bartzella' AGM, an intersectional peony which offers huge bright yellow flowers to boot.

For more scented peonies, consider *Paeonia lactiflora* 'Alexander Fleming' (double rose-pink), *Paeonia lactiflora* 'Honey Gold' (single white with golden-yellow centre), *Paeonia lactiflora* 'Boule de Neige' (double creamy white 'snowballs'), *Paeonia lactiflora* 'Lady Alexandra Duff' (double sugar pink), or my favourite, *Paeonia lactiflora* 'Catharina Fontijn', which has very soft pink, almost blush double flowers. An excellent late-season scented peony is *Paeonia lactiflora* 'Sarah Bernhardt' AGM (double rose pink with darker flares), an old favourite, but one which will reliably flower later than

Remember that peonies are most likely to be fragrant first thing in the morning and early in the day, when the morning sun awakens them, and as the day progresses their scent will evaporate and diminish.

many others. For fragrant red peonies, look for *Paeonia lactiflora* 'Inspecteur Lavergne' (double crimson red), *Paeonia lactiflora* 'Big Ben' (dark red bomb shape), *Paeonia* 'Christmas Velvet' (dark red, fully double) or *Paeonia* 'Diana Parks' (bright red and very beautiful). There are many, many more, however, and it seems an injustice to highlight only these few varieties.

The perfume of peonies is a key part of what makes them so important and valued to us – smells and scents evoke memories and are inextricably linked because of the brain's anatomy. The perfume of peonies is very subjective, however, as each of us perceive scent in a different way. Beware, though, of a small number of peonies whose fragrance is not particularly pleasant, the popular and very attractive *Paeonia* 'Coral Charm' AGM, for example, because although these peonies do indeed possess a perfume, they are not necessarily pleasantly fragrant and (I do not wish to be indelicate here) are commonly described as 'fishy'. Thankfully, these peonies are relatively small in number and very much the exception. The overwhelming majority of peonies will impress, inspire and enchant you with their fragrances.

Remember that peonies are most likely to be fragrant first thing in the morning and early in the day, when the morning sun awakens them, and as the day progresses their scent will evaporate and diminish. The temperature will therefore affect the fragrance of peonies, as will the age of the plant (and the age of the bloom), so remember to feed your peony every few years or so.

The heavenly fragrance of peonies is unique and not easily replicated in man-made perfumes. Obtaining natural peony oils is exceptionally difficult, therefore it has to be the real thing, and there is nothing like it.

Top left: *Paeonia* 'Bartzella' AGM is a wonderful semi-double intersectional peony with a fragrance.

Top right: *Paeonia lactiflora* 'Lady Alexandra Duff'.

Bottom left: *Paeonia lactiflora* 'Big Ben'.

Bottom right: *Paeonia lactiflora* 'Alexander Fleming'.

Fragrant Peonies

Here are a small selection of my favourites:

Albert Crousse
Alexander Fleming
Alice Harding
Avalanche
Baroness Schroeder
Big Ben
Boule de Neige
Bridal Icing
Bridal Shower
Catharina Fontijn
Christmas Velvet

Claire de Lune AGM
Diana Parks
Duchesse de Nemours AGM
Eden's Perfume
Edulis Superba
Etched Salmon
Festiva Maxima AGM
Florence Nicholls AGM
Gardenia
High Noon AGM
Honey Gold

Immaculee AGM
Kelway's Glorious AGM
Lady Alexandra Duff
Lady Anna
Laura Dessert
Lorelei
Lotus Queen
Love Affair
Madame Calot
Margaret Truman
Marie Lemoine

mlokosewitschii AGM
Monsieur Jules Elie AGM
Nancy Nora AGM
Peter Brand
Pink Parfait
Primevere
Sarah Bernhardt AGM
Shirley Temple AGM
White Wings

Musky Sweet Rose Citrus Spicy

Top left: *Paeonia lactiflora* 'Festiva Maxima' AGM.

Top right: *Paeonia lactiflora* 'Pink Parfait'.

Bottom left: *Paeonia lactiflora* 'Peter Brand'.

Bottom right: *Paeonia lactiflora* 'Lady Anna'.

Pages 156-157: Mixed perennial border with peonies, Wrest Park, Bedfordshire.

Common Myths about Peonies

Peonies herald the call for the start of summer, epitomising the fun and joy the season brings, their riot of colour and gorgeous fragrance filling the air with sweet, spicy and lemon scents. You can't help but smile when you see peony buds start to form – the anticipation of them blooming heightens the senses and fills one with all the eagerness of a child waiting to open their presents on Christmas morning.

For some, though, long-held myths about growing peonies have stopped them from choosing to grow these wonderful and virtually care-free plants in their garden.

Myth 1: Peonies are hard to grow

This myth is the most prolific and the truth is if you follow some simple rules with peonies you will be able to have a gorgeous plant blooming in your garden from the first season you plant it.

1. Buy a well-established, mature peony plant (peonies don't flower reliably until they are around five years old).

2. Plant in a sheltered sunny or part shaded position in any free-draining soil.

3. Don't plant your herbaceous or intersectional peony too deep – ensure the crown is no more than 25mm below the surface. Over mulching is a common cause for a peony failing to flower.

4. Feed your peony plant once a year in the spring or autumn.

5. Cut back herbaceous and intersectional peonies in the autumn, once the leaves have turned brown; remember, woody peonies respond well to pruning to keep them under control.

6. Water your peony consistently while buds are forming in the spring, but take care not to overwater, as peonies don't like to have wet 'feet', or roots.

Peonies herald the call for the start of summer, epitomising the fun and joy the season brings.

Left: Scented peonies in the border at Penshurst Place and Gardens, Kent.

Myth 2: Peonies are delicate and don't like the cold

It's not clear exactly where this myth has come from, but a lot of peony beginners have been worried about the more recent cold and snowy winters. The truth is that parts of China and Japan, well known for woody peonies, have much colder climates, yet peonies have been popular there for centuries and used in medicine and food for thousands of years. There are also well-known growers and breeders in northern states in the USA, and even in Alaska, very well known for lots of snow! Peonies are hardy down to about -20°c and enjoy the colder weather, which signals a dormant period above ground where buds form on the roots below the surface, ready to re-emerge when the weather starts to heat up towards spring. Most growers will tell you that the colder the winter, the better the blooms the following spring.

A late frost can sometimes cause damage but won't do any lasting harm to the plant. If you are worried, you can cover your peonies with some netting or straw to prevent the frost settling.

Myth 3: Peonies will only grow in certain soil types

Myth totally busted: peonies are happy in pretty much any soil type, even clay, provided the soil is fertile and free draining. If you have particularly solid clay soil, try mixing some sand or organic matter through the soil to encourage drainage before planting and ensure there is sufficient drainage at the bottom of the planting hole. When planting a new peony in the garden it is always a good idea to add some fertiliser to assist root growth for the first season. You can continue to feed your peony once a year, and while this is not essential, it can encourage stronger plants and better blooms.

Myth 4: Peonies cannot be moved

A few bad experiences and maybe inexperience have promoted this myth about peonies. Peonies, once established, will prefer to remain in one spot (provided it has sufficient space and sunlight) and, a bit like us gardeners, will not be terribly happy

Most growers will tell you that the colder the winter, the better the blooms the following spring.

Right: Penshurst Place and Gardens, Kent.

There are a couple of things to be aware of when replanting a peony – these are usually the cause of the plant not flowering the following year.

about being moved from the cosy spot to which it has become accustomed, but peonies are absolutely fine with being moved. It is best to plan where you would like to move your peony to ensure as smooth a transition as possible. The best time is also in the autumn, once the plant has been cut back (and pruned if it is a woody peony) and is dormant.

There are a couple of things to be aware of when replanting a peony – these are usually the cause of the plant not flowering the following year. Firstly, ensure the eyes (the pink buds on the roots) are not damaged in lifting, transport or replanting. Secondly, ensure that the plant has not been buried or covered with too much soil – a herbaceous peony crown needs to be quite close to the surface, only approximately 2.5-5cm deep (also be cautious when mulching your borders that you don't cover up the base of your peony). The process is the same when planting woody peonies, but with grafted peonies it is best to plant them with the graft union about 10-15cm below the surface. Finally, remember that when replanting the peony requires plenty of space and sunlight to thrive.

Myth 5: Peonies only last for a few years like normal perennials

This could not be further from the truth and may have come about because a recently acquired peony may not have flowered and people think they have essentially died, dug them up and not given them a chance.

Peonies are in fact a long-lived plant. They can last for decades in the garden and some varieties have been known to live for 100 plus years happily. Peonies take a while to mature from seedling or cutting and so plants tend to only flower at three to five years old. To have the best success with peonies, buy mature plants from a reputable nursery – a mature peony should bloom in your garden from the very first year and continue to produce more and more blooms every year. If you see or have a peony with twenty to thirty blooms, tip your hat and salute, as it may be older than you!

Left: Peonies in the walled garden at Fenton House, London.

Myth 6: Fragrant? Really?

Some varieties are more fragrant than others, but peonies are most certainly scented. There are different types of peony scent, many ranging from spicy and sweet to powdery and citrus, and for the best peony perfumes it is best to look for semi-double and double blooms. Many of the older varieties were bred specifically to create fragrance and some peonies have very strong perfumes.

Myth 7: Peonies only flower in May

While individual plants may often flower for only a few weeks each year, with careful selection of cultivars you could have peonies flowering in your garden from April through to July.

Hopefully I have been able to solve a few common problems and concerns about these stunning and popular flowering plants to encourage you to grow them in your own garden – be confident! They are tough plants and require little care compared to some of their thornier garden compatriots. They are forgiving, so if you currently own a peony that is underperforming, you can and should be able to solve its issues. With all their varieties, sizes, flower shapes, colours and fragrances, there is surely a peony for everyone, and every garden deserves at least one peony.

There are different types of peony scent, ranging from spicy, sweet, powdery and citrus, and for the best peony perfumes it is best to look for semi-double and double blooms.

Right: *Paeonia lactiflora* 'Germain Bigot'.

Pages 166-167: *Paeonia mascula* subsp. *arietina*, Waterperry House and Gardens, Oxfordshire.

The Stars of the Show

I have been fascinated by flower shows ever since my teenage visits to RHS Hampton Court Palace Flower Show with my grandmother.

Flower shows have been popular in the UK since the early 1800s, providing entertainment and inspiration for generations of gardeners and enthusiasts.

Competition is a key part of exhibiting, and putting together displays and exhibits presents particular challenges for growers and nurserymen in addition to the day-to-day work of growing plants and operating a commercial nursery. From planning, designing and building exciting exhibits to the painstaking endeavour required to grow exhibition-quality plants with the English weather, as well as the very long, tiring, but incredibly enjoyable days attending the show, exhibiting can really take over your life and is in some ways a lifestyle choice.

I have been fascinated by flower shows ever since my teenage visits to RHS Hampton Court Palace Flower Show with my grandmother. Although I entered the local horticultural flower and produce show annually, I never imagined that one day I would exhibit at prestigious events (including RHS Hampton Court Palace itself), alongside some of the finest growers and exhibitors in the country, let alone be awarded Gold Medals. Exhibiting for me has been a dream come true.

Of course, in reality exhibiting is far from being a dream, requiring a lot of hard work (it can be physically very demanding) and a sustained and high level of concentration and dedication, not to mention a lot of time away from home and the family.

I love the challenge of creating innovative, interesting and engaging displays to highlight our very best plants and blooms, and there is always a sense of excitement (and dread) when it comes to judging. Although winning medals is not everything (visitor enjoyment and personal satisfaction and pride in your own work is far more rewarding), it is deeply pleasing when the exhibit and the plants are judged to be worthy of a Gold Medal. Exhibiting also provides an excellent opportunity to generate awareness, and to promote peonies and talk to the thousands of visitors, many of whom are keen gardeners and have fascinating stories to tell.

Left: Model wears a peony headress, RHS Chelsea Flower Show 2017.

Above: Chelsea Pensioners enjoying themselves at RHS Chelsea Flower Show 2019.

Top left: RHS Chelsea Flower Show 2017 – 'Exploring the Fragrance of Peonies'.

Top right: RHS Chelsea 2018 – 'Love is in the Mind'.

Bottom left: RHS Chelsea 2019 – 'Love Peonies'.

Bottom right: RHS Chelsea Flower Show 2022 – 'The Enchanting Peony'.

I started exhibiting properly in 2012 but had to wait until 2015 before I was invited to exhibit in the floral marquee. The first exhibit I staged here was ambitious and, if I am totally honest, it received a mixed reaction – it was the creation of a nightclub, the idea being that the exhibit would be separated into two parts, with visitors first walking through an enclosed nightclub before exiting through a 'chill-out' zone. This involved the erection of a 4m square exhibit with 2.4m high walls and a pathway through the centre. Externally it was said to look like a toilet block in the middle of the marquee, but inside it was a thrilling and exciting space, complete with music, dancefloor, coloured lights and, of course, lots of alstroemeria plants. The chill-out zone was brighter and more relaxed, with a day bed, candles and plenty of beautiful peonies. We were awarded a Silver-Gilt medal and I was delighted to receive such a high award on my first attempt, as well as it being great fun and a useful learning experience. From that point on we had decided that our exhibits would be different, contemporary and innovative, which has meant a mixed bag in terms of medal awards. Judging sometimes struggles to keep up with visitor expectations and would often rather see a more traditional exhibit with row after row of uniform, perfect blooms in vases. The public response to our exhibits has always been incredible, though, regardless of the medal awarded.

In what was a relatively unusual move, the RHS invited me to the Grand Pavilion at RHS Chelsea Flower Show the following year as part of their innovation programme to encourage creative and bold exhibits. The RHS Chelsea Flower Show is generally held in May each year, the perfect time for exhibiting peonies, and has taken place in the grounds of the Royal Hospital, Chelsea since 1912. I was pleased to be fast-tracked into such a prestigious flower show but also quite daunted, not least because of my floral marquee inexperience, as RHS Chelsea Flower Show is often seen as representing the very pinnacle of success in horticulture. I was very much aware of the history and weight of expectation.

Left: HM Queen Elizabeth II visiting our exhibit and talking to me at RHS Chelsea Flower Show 2022. © Paul Grover.

Our exhibit in 2016, for which I was mentored by multi-award-winning Chelsea Gold medallist Kate Gould, whose advice and encouragement was invaluable, was awarded a Silver medal. I had decided to focus on the luxurious, decadent and beautiful peony blooms and designed a background exhibit with a wall of peonies on one side, a chaise longue surrounded by a mass of peony plants in full bloom and a modern, custom-made chandelier from which I could hang cut flower peonies (although when it came to building the exhibit the chaise longue turned out to be more of a foot stool, which then meant frantic efforts to locate a suitable chaise longue late on a Friday afternoon, two days before judging). The entire exhibit was a mass of colour and scent, overwhelming the senses, and quite a risk; I don't think peonies had ever been shown in such a contemporary and conceptual way before, generally being displayed in a garden or traditional vase type setting. Although it was quite a small exhibit (I think 4m long by 1.8m deep), it took mum, dad and I three days to put together. We were the last people in the pavilion each night, working on top of each other to complete it. RHS Chelsea Flower Show is very tight for space and the logistics of simply getting the van on site takes some getting used to, easily delaying your day's work by several hours. On the positive side, the more experienced exhibitors were very kind and generous with their time and advice, and I am very thankful and grateful for their support. In the end it was an incredibly tiring but fabulous week, and I can still recall the thronging crowds of visitors massing around the exhibit and asking every question about peonies you could imagine.

In 2017 my RHS Chelsea Flower Show exhibit focused on the fragrance of peonies and I moved a step closer to achieving my ambition, winning a Silver-Gilt medal. We created some peony headdresses for the press day event, and with a paparazzi-style bank of photographers covering the exhibit they were photographed a lot and used in newspapers, magazines and online. Behind the scenes, however, the models were very wet and complained (not unreasonably) about the weight of the headdresses, which had been built around wet oasis flower foam.

I started exhibiting properly in 2012 but had to wait until 2015 before I was able to exhibit in the floral marquee.

Right: Our first exhibit in 2016 at RHS Chelsea Flower Show celebrated the decadence and indulgence of peonies.

By 2018, I was feeling a little bit more confident about exhibiting and our RHS Chelsea Flower Show entry that year was a much larger walk-through exhibit. As usual, my dad and my uncle Philip did the building over a four-day period, erecting a 2.4m high moss wall studded with cut flower peonies to frame a contemporary sculpture commissioned for the exhibit from a local sculptor, amongst other things. Again, my exhibit focused on peonies as a symbol of love and romance and I was able to use masses of them. We were awarded a Silver-Gilt, which, at the time, I thought was a little hard. Overall, the show was fabulous, and the exhibit received an incredible response from visitors.

Following the success of 2018, I was keen to try something slightly larger and more dramatic at RHS Chelsea Flower Show in spring 2019. Sticking with the decadent luxury of peonies, I again designed a walk-though exhibit, featuring neon lights, clear Perspex cubes lit with bright lights, smoke machines and a bath filled with peonies. I tried to make sure that the exhibit contained plants that had rarely been seen at flower shows (or at all) in the UK and so included a lot of intersectional cultivars in the display. The build took an entire week and involved, at times, more than a dozen people. We had decided to create a 'river' of peonies flowing down from the back wall of the exhibit into the bath and my mum and Andy (our talented florist) spent hours creating the framework and carefully placing each and every one of the hundreds of peony blooms. The attention to detail required is immense and the judges somehow manage to always find the one hole that wasn't filled or the bare underside of the floral arrangements. On top of everything else, there are the plants to consider – peonies can be very temperamental when it comes to flowering, and the flower, when it opens, does not always last very long. It is therefore a nerve-wracking experience waiting to find out if the blooms will open in time for judging (by which time it is too late to do anything about it). Judging at RHS Chelsea Flower Show is usually carried out by experienced panels who start in the floral marquee around 7am, a little early for the peonies, which often don't open fully until mid to late morning, when the temperature has warmed up a little and the sun has emerged. The floral marquee is also a strange

Top left: Model with hand-painted peonies and a fresh headpiece at RHS Chelsea Flower Show 2019, which caused a bit of a stir.

Top right: Alec surrounded by models wearing designer wedding dresses with peony crowns and bouquets as wedding flowers. RHS Chelsea Flower Show 2018.

Bottom right: Our huge peony hand-made head dresses for press day at RHS Chelsea Flower Show 2017 which gained international attention.

place to exhibit flowers as the light is quite odd (which after a few days can affect the blooms themselves) and it can be very humid and warm, which again is not always conducive to maintaining exhibition-quality blooms.

Again, we were one of the last groups to leave the floral marquee the night before judging, but to add to the pressure we also had a disaster. We had two large, 1.2m high glass vases which held a cut flower peony display that were to be mounted atop two large Perspex cubes either side of the front of the display. We had carefully chosen these vases and sourced them as a pair (from a selection of just three) from the back of the dusty stockroom of a wholesaler. For some reason the vases had been temporarily placed on the ground (I think it was so that we could cover the underside of the bowl containing the cut flower display so that it couldn't be seen through the glass vase), and as the helper who was sweeping the grass turned around, she knocked the vase and in slow-motion reached out to catch it as it fell to the ground. The vase smashed into a thousand pieces, leaving us with a very one-sided exhibit. It was about 8pm on Sunday evening and we had no option but to rise bright and early the next day to drive to the wholesaler at 4am. In a stroke of luck, we were able to purchase the last remaining matching glass vase and navigate through the centre of London back to the show ground to finish the exhibit before judging at 7am. It was fraught and we were all tired, but we just about finished before the judges arrived. Once this was completed, the press arrived and we had a busy morning trying to make the most of the unique marketing opportunity that RHS Chelsea Flower Show presents, followed by the royal visit of HM The Queen to the floral marquee and then the Gala Evening, which finished at around 9pm. It was a long and tiring day and as interesting and glamorous as the press day is, replete with celebrities and television, it is the plants that are the stars of the show, and I was eagerly awaiting the result of the judging to see how my plants had done.

The following morning, which is when the medals are awarded, I was completely exhausted as I approached the exhibit, noticed the medal card and wasn't particularly surprised to find myself thinking, 'Oh, another Silver-Gilt' as I passed by on my way to

Again, we were one of the last groups to leave the floral marquee the night before judging, but to add to the pressure we also had a disaster.

Right: Our first RHS Chelsea Flower Show Gold Medal-winning exhibit from 2019, including magnificent arrangements atop matching glass vases.

It takes a year or more to plan a Chelsea exhibit and many months of attentive care to ensure the plants are in the best condition possible for exhibition.

my morning cup of tea. It was only when I returned and actually looked at the award that I noticed it was a Gold medal – the first Gold awarded for a peony exhibit at RHS Chelsea Flower Show for eight years. I was stunned but so pleased at this well-deserved recognition for the wider team, whose efforts helped grow the plants throughout the year as well as building and erecting the exhibit.

The global COVID pandemic meant that flower shows in 2020 were cancelled and seriously reduced in number in 2021. We have been awarded Gold Medals since for our exhibits but our first RHS Gold will always be extra special to me.

It takes a year or more to plan a Chelsea exhibit and many months of attentive care to ensure the plants are in the best condition possible for exhibition. To achieve this, we will regularly move plants into warmer polytunnels and then back out again to regulate the progress of bud development, as well as using our cold storage unit to delay or slow down growth. From time to time we will put peonies in a cold, dark room to hold flower buds back from opening or indeed put them in the house to encourage them to open. There is a lot of moving plants around the nursery, sometimes just from a sunny position to a shadier one and vice versa. We will often disbud and remove the side buds on exhibition plants whilst giving them a little more space to grow and perhaps an extra feed or two. Some of our exhibition plants are several years old and we have around 3,000 of them in total, simply because we can never be quite sure which ones will be ready in time for each flower show in the season. Getting the peonies to flower at the right time in sufficient quantities is always worrying for me, while my dad tends to worry about whether the ground inside the floral marquee is level – getting a level base for the exhibit seems to be one of the hardest things to achieve!

Flower shows are marvellous simply because of the range of plants on display, many of which will be unusual and rarely seen, and the availability of expert advice and knowledge from the various specialist growers. They are a great source of inspiration for gardeners and the perfect place for growers, like me, to reach a wider audience and share our passion for the plants we grow.

Left: Our interactive educational exhibit, sponsored by Theo Fennell at the September RHS Chelsea Flower Show 2021, including flower blooms that we preserved in resin.

As a result of the pandemic restrictions, in 2021 RHS Chelsea Flower Show was held in September for the first time, which presented us with an obvious difficulty: peonies do not flower in the UK in September. Prior to the pandemic, we had planned, with leading jeweller Theo Fennell, to put forward a large, extravagant walk-though exhibit to showcase the skills and craftsmanship of the master jeweller and the expertise and endeavour required to grow the finest peonies. Our plans had been over a year in the making and Theo Fennell had designed and made a gorgeous peony ring which was to be the centre-piece of the exhibit. But with the flower show being held in September and without any peonies to put in the exhibit our plans had to be radically changed and we were sadly unable to proceed as planned. Instead we put together an educational display to illustrate the great artistry and skill of peony growers and master jewellers, in an exhibit called 'Treasure Every Moment'. It was one of the most technically challenging exhibits I have ever put together and it was important to ensure that visitors could engage with it in different ways, so we had video of the plants growing in the nursery, flower blooms preserved in resin, peonies showing autumn foliage, rotating exhibits and, of course, the peony ring itself.

We returned to a walk-though exhibit for RHS Chelsea Flower Show in May 2022, using photography from a photoshoot we had on the nursery in 2021 and set in a woodland scene, called 'The Enchanted Peony'. With a swing surrounded by peonies I wanted the exhibit to have a magical and enchanting feel, allowing visitors to get much closer to the peony blooms as they walked along the meandering woodland path through the exhibit. The display contained over 1,000 peony plants and was the largest peony exhibit we have ever built. We were delighted to be awarded a Silver medal and I was even more thrilled and honoured to be chosen to meet HM Queen Elizabeth II and talk to her about our peonies during the royal visit.

As a result of the pandemic restrictions, for the first time, RHS Chelsea Flower Show was held in September 2021 which presented us with an obvious difficulty; peonies do not flower in the UK in September.

Right: 'The Enchanting Peony', our exhibit at RHS Chelsea Flower Show 2022.

Propagation

Propagating peonies is relatively easy (although it is of course much quicker to simply purchase a mature peony from a nursery for effortless, instant results). Peonies are usually, but not always, propagated by either division of peony roots or from seed.

Peonies are usually, but not always, propagated by either division of peony roots or from seed.

Both methods are straight forward and the approach taken may depend on your desired outcome. For example, seed-raised peonies require a lot of patience and often do not produce offspring that are the same as the parent, but this can be desirable and exciting because it is likely that an entirely new variety will be produced. Root division will, however, sometimes produce a copy of the mother plant that will establish more quickly in the garden, which is perfect if you are looking to replicate the characteristics of the mother plant. Peonies can also be propagated by root cuttings, grafting, softwood cuttings and by micro-propagation (tissue culture), though these methods are not normally adopted by gardeners and are used predominantly by commercial growers.

Description of roots, crown and 'eyes'

Peony roots can be big and chunky, but when the plant is young the roots are often slim and slender. The 'crown' is the part of the peony root that is at the top of the root and it is from the crown that the plant's stems come, at the base of the plant. As the plant matures the tuberous peony roots will get larger, storing greater quantities of food for the plant whilst lots of creamy-white, fibrous or hairy roots that are attached to the fat, tuberous roots spread out into the soil and take up water and nutrients.

Mature, established peony roots will have a number of buds or 'eyes' on them, usually around the crown and the largest buds will develop underground and will be shoots in the Spring providing above-ground growth that will become stems bearing leaves and flower buds. The buds are pretty tough and hardy but when they emerge through the surface of the soil in the Spring the shoots can sometimes be damaged by severe frosts or sustained wet weather.

Left: On the nursery we grow peonies both outside in standing out beds and also in a number of large polyethylene tunnels. In general, the peonies in the tunnels tend to flower earlier than outside.

Dividing peonies

Although peonies do not need to be regularly divided for their own benefit, it may be desirable to divide a peony that has got too big for the space available or to create more peony plants for the garden. Peonies that have been divided recover well, but note the obvious point that the larger the division of peony the more quickly it will recover and flower again. Whether dividing herbaceous, intersectional or woody peonies it is best to wait until the plant is around three to five years old and is sufficiently established before attempting to make divisions. Beware though, because older peonies (especially woody peonies) can get quite large making division particularly difficult.

Herbaceous peonies

Lift the peony plant carefully and without damaging the roots; the tuberous roots can easily snap and break and the whitish aerial roots are quite delicate. Brush away as much soil from the roots as possible without damaging the roots because this will enable you to see exactly what you are doing. Using either a sharp spade or, if the plant is smaller, a knife, cut the root into the desired number of pieces (or 'divisions'), ensuring that each division has at least three to five eyes or buds and a substantial fat tuberous root (that is full of food and energy) to sustain the division once replanted. Cut away any infected or rotten roots and discard. Replant the division in either another part of the garden or in a container. Remember to carefully water the peony the following year because the root system will not be fully developed and to avoid overwatering, which may rot the crown of the root.

Woody or tree peonies

Propagation of woody peonies by division can be slightly more tricky but in essence the process is the same as when dividing herbaceous or intersectional peonies. Once lifted from the ground it will be necessary to carefully inspect the root of the woody peony and to identify where the divisions should be made to ensure that each division has three to five 'eyes' (which could be above-ground on the stem or below ground on the root system) and healthy, tuberous roots. Once divided, prune the stems back to leave

Although peonies do not need to be regularly divided for their own benefit it may be desirable to divide a peony that has got too big for the space available.

Top left: Bare-root peonies lifted in autumn, ready for potting.

Top right: Early stages of propagation with seed trays containing peony seeds.

Bottom left: Peony seedling.

Bottom right: Whole peony plant with root and top growth.

between three and five buds and be prepared to wait a year or two to see blooms on the plant because divisions of woody peonies often don't flower the following year.

Growing from seed

Growing peonies from seed requires some patience and dedication but it is well worthwhile and an enchanting method to adopt when propagating peonies. Peonies raised from seed may take five or more years to flower and seedlings can be vulnerable to pests and diseases. Many of the garden cultivars and hybrid peonies do not produce viable seed and can only be reproduced through division. Germinating seed from species peonies is relatively easy though. There is always a high degree of excitement and anticipation because seed-raised peonies in the garden rarely produce plants that are true to type, that is to say, the seed-raised plant may or may not look like the plant that produced the seed and a new peony created with a different flower colour, flower shape or growth habit. The reason for this is natural cross-pollination of flowers from bees and other pollinators, which is more likely where there are several peonies nearby (either in your garden or a neighbour's garden). Peony seeds are generally quite large and simple to harvest and sow (this also makes them easy to see). Fertilised seed is usually a dark brown or bluish black.

As the seed ages, the outer coating becomes harder and the seed becomes slower to germinate, sometimes taking two years, which is part of the secret of these long-lived plants, enabling the seed to lie dormant in the soil until the conditions are optimal for growth. For the best results, sowing fresh seed in early autumn is recommended because fresh seed will usually germinate straight away.

Plant fresh seed immediately into a well-prepared flower bed or well-drained, gritty and open soil-based compost in a seed tray or pot in the late summer. Place the seeds in the seed tray or pot and cover with about 2.5cm of soil. Place the seed tray or pot outside in the garden in a cold frame or sheltered position. Lightly water the seed tray or pot and cover with alpine grit. If you do not have a cold frame, keep a close eye on the seed tray or pot to ensure that it does not become over watered. Freshly sown seed

Peonies raised from seed may take five or more years to flower and seedlings can be vulnerable to pests and diseases.

Freshly sown seed will usually germinate the following spring, with the roots beginning to develop, but often above-ground growth will not appear until the following year, so it is important to be patient.

will usually germinate the following spring, with the roots beginning to develop, but often above-ground growth will not appear until the following year, so it is important to be patient even though it may look as if the seeds have not germinated immediately. Once germinated, take extra special care with your seedlings for a year or two because they are especially vulnerable to attack by slugs and snails. Once the seedling is a couple of years or more old, it will generally survive any mollusc assault.

If you are sowing slightly older peony seeds that have dried out or seeds that have been harvested later in the season, you may find the germination is less reliable than with freshly sown seed. This is because the seed becomes dormant (part of its survival strategy) and it may need longer to germinate, sometimes up to two years. There are techniques to speed up the process, including placing the seed in a fridge or cold-store for a period of time to trick the seed into breaking its dormancy and germinating sooner. Place the seed in a sealable plastic bag to retain moisture together with some moss or perlite and place the bag in a warm, dark place for about eight to ten weeks. Keep an eye on the seeds and, in time, you should see germination. The seeds will produce very fine, white rootlets. Once the rootlets are about 2" long (or about a finger's length), place the sealed plastic bags in the fridge (set the temperature around 3-4°C) for a further three or four months. After the refrigeration period, carefully disentangle the roots and plant into pots of open, free-draining compost for a year or two before planting out in the garden. Regularly lightly water the young seedlings to keep them moist but not overwatered.

Remember that the flowers of a young, immature peony are not necessarily the same as the flowers of the same plant when it matures, at around five years old. Therefore, expect to see peculiar colours or shapes of bloom that will change and crystallise into their final form and colour as the plant matures.

The Peony in Art and Culture

Used to adorn imperial palaces, peonies were often displayed in reception halls and utilised in large vases as a table plant.

Origins of the peony

Long before their introduction to the west, peonies were wild plants which originated in the barren region of Shaanxi in northwestern China. Their use in a medicinal context began some 2,000 years ago, with the roots commonly used in Traditional Chinese Medicine as a treatment for pain and swelling and as an antioxidant, among other purposes, but by the 6th and 7th centuries AD the tree peony was being cultivated for its flowers, namely during the Sui (581-618 AD) and Tang dynasties (618-906 AD). Used to adorn imperial palaces, peonies were often displayed in reception halls and utilised in large vases as a table plant, placing the peony among the first flowers to be cultivated for ornamental purposes. As a result, the ancient city of Luòyáng, the seat of the Sung dynasty (960-1279 AD), became one of the centres of this practice, and peonies are often referred to as *luòyànghuā*, or 'flower from Luòyáng' – a festival dedicated to them, discussed later in this chapter, is still held annually in the city.

During this period the historian, writer and poet Ouyang Xiu (1007-1072) composed the *Luoyang mudan ji*, or *Peonies of Luoyang*, a treatise which contains the first written Chinese description of garden flowers and records the shift from their medicinal use to being decorative plants. The enthusiasm for peonies during the Sung dynasty can be compared to the boom in the cultivation of tulips that occurred in Holland during the 17th century, and highly prized peonies commanded large prices. While the growing of *Paeonia officinalis* began in Europe from the 15th century onwards and the tree peony was introduced at Kew Gardens in 1789, intensive breeding only began during the 19th century, with the introduction of *Paeonia lactiflora.*

Left: This early 15th-century example of a Chinese carved lacquer dish features two peafowls flying amid blossoming peonies. The motif of a pair of birds among flowers also became a standard design for other media, such as textiles and ceramics, especially between the 13th and 15th centuries, and were produced by the imperial workshop of the Ming dynasty (1368-1644).

The legend of how the peony became the Queen of Flowers

This account provides a more legendary or speculative explanation for the reverence of peonies in China:

Ruling between 684-704 AD during the Tang Dynasty, Empress Wu Zetian, on seeing how devoid of colour her royal gardens were during the winter, issued an imperial decree that all the flowers there must bloom in midwinter. On hearing this, the flower fairies knew that such a demand would force them to go against nature, but none dared to defy the Empress. The garden was soon in full bloom, even under heavy falling snow, and this pleased Wu Zetian as she admired her power. Only one flower had refused her – the peony. The Empress ordered all the peonies in the capital of Luoyang to be burned in an act of revenge, but amongst the flames their colour appeared even more striking. To the surprise of the residents, when spring came the peonies had returned and were able to bloom once more. For this the flower fairies named the peony the 'Queen of Flowers', with the tale used to illustrate that the right path is not always the easiest to take.

Luoyang Gardens Peony Festival

The Luoyang Gardens Peony Festival takes place annually in the city from 15-25 April, when peonies are in full bloom and generally reaching their peak appearance, and is the largest festival in the world dedicated to the flower. One of several celebrated flower fairs in China, the festival is an important site of cultural heritage and a huge attraction for peony enthusiasts globally. During the festival, gardens are awash with peonies of all colours, with folk performances also staged during the festival. The poem 'The Blossoms of Luoyang' by Ting Liunang, written during the Tang Dynasty (618-907 AD), is one testament to the heritage of the city.

The Empress ordered all the peonies in the capital of Luoyang to be burned in an act of revenge, but amongst the flames their colour appeared even more striking.

Above: Thousands flock to Luoyang each year
for the Peoony Festival, the largest of its kind
in the world.

> From originally being reserved for royalty and the aristocracy and seen as representative of this societal status, their cultivation eventually spread throughout China.

The Blossoms of Luoyang

My lover is like the tree peony of Luoyang,

I, unworthy, like the common willows of Wu Chang.

Both places love the spring wind.

When shall we hold each other's hands again?

Incessant the buzzing of insects beyond the orchard curtain.

The moon flings slanting shadows from the pepper tree across the courtyard.

Pity the girl of the flowery house, who is not equal to the blossoms of Luoyang.

Etymological myths

Two more mythological tales attest to how the peony got its name. In the first, according to Greek mythology, Paeon, the physician to the gods, was able to cure Pluto's ailment by using an extract from the root of a peony. Asclepius, god of medicine and healing, was angered at this perceived slight on his own abilities and threatened the life of Paeon, his student. Fortunately for him, Paeon was saved by Zeus, who turned him into the peony flower.

A second myth ties the name to the nymph Paeonia, who attracted the god Apollo with her beauty. For spite rather than for protection in this case, Aphrodite turned the blushing-red nymph into a peony. This story is also likely what led to the peony being associated with poor luck during the Victorian period and the resulting superstition that it was unlucky to dig up a peony.

Symbolism and meaning

Along with some of the many other flowers grown in China, the peony has a long history of symbolic meaning. From originally being reserved for royalty and the aristocracy and seen as representative of this societal status, their cultivation eventually spread throughout China. The ink and deep red forms, as well as a variety with a yellow edge on the petals, known as the 'golden border peony', were highly valued. The peony is also called *fùguìhūa*, the flower (*hūa*) of wealth (*fù*) and rank (*guì*).

Left: Detail of a silk hanging scroll depicting peacocks and peonies by Tani Bunchō (1763-1840). Painted in 1820, this Japanese example demonstrates how Bunchō learned the pictorial vocabulary of birds and flowers from earlier Chinese painters while in service there, with the peacock and peonies used here to represent power and wealth.

Despite being associated with the yang principle (male) of masculinity and brightness, peonies are also understood to represent female beauty and reproduction.

In Serbian culture and folklore, the red flowers of *Paeonia peregrina*, known as Kosovo peonies, are seen to represent the blood shed by Serbian warriors killed during the Battle of Kosovo, which took place in 1389 between the Serbian prince Lazar Hrebeljanović and the invading forces of the Ottoman Empire. In some Eastern European countries, the peony is associated with modesty and shyness, likely tied to the story of the nymph Paeonia.

During the Middle Ages Christians considered the peony plant a symbol of wealth, beauty, and health, commonly using the roots and seeds in herbal teas and medicines. Many of these Christians started creating hybrids in hope of increasing the potency of its curative abilities.

A representative flower

The peony has been used as the representative flower for countries and states, especially their native China, and has subsequently appeared in various forms, from public art to stamps. The peony is still overwhelmingly popular and considered as the national flower there today, topping all other contenders in a 2019 vote with 79.7 percent; the plum blossom came in a distant second, with 12.3 percent. In 1957, the Indiana General Assembly passed a law to make the peony the state flower of Indiana, a title which it holds to this day.

The peony in art

With longstanding symbolic associations, peonies have been a traditional floral symbol in eastern art, appearing in numerous forms over the centuries. Artists in both China and Japan have made wide use of the peony as a motif, featuring it in paintings, on porcelain, as a design in embroidered clothing, on screen paintings and tapestries. Contemporary paintings in the Chinese style continue to utilise the peony design, along with other popular subjects such as birds and bamboo. In visual art the peony is

Above: The peony has been used as a representative flower by many nations – these stamps are from Latvia and Romania respectively.

Notable European painters of peonies have included Édouard Manet, who created a series of still life pictures of the flower during 1864-65, including Peonies in a Vase on a Stand.

used to symbolise a number of qualities, including prosperity, riches, honour, love and affection. Peonies are also a common subject in tattoos, often used along with koi-fish. The popular use of peonies in Japanese tattoo art was inspired by the ukiyo-e artist Utagawa Kuniyoshi's illustrations of Suikoden, a classical Chinese novel. His paintings of warrior-heroes covered in pictorial tattoos included lions, tigers, dragons, koi fish, and peonies, among other symbols. The peony became a masculine motif, associated with a devil-may-care attitude and disregard for consequence.

Notable European painters of peonies have included Édouard Manet, who created a series of still life pictures of the flower during 1864-65, including *Peonies in a Vase on a Stand*. This example was also an influence on Vincent Van Gogh, who on viewing the picture commented that this 'very extraordinary' piece appeared 'as much a flower as anything could be'; it also served as inspiration for Van Gogh's own series of flower paintings during this period. Though Van Gogh describes the peonies as 'pink', the quality of the painting's colour has unfortunately been lost due to the deterioration of the pigments used and as a result they now appear white. A relatively recent addition to European flora at this time, peonies were a luxury item that appealed as a subject to Manet's patrons; he even grew them himself in his garden at Gennevilliers. Other renowned artists to utilise the peony as their subject include Claude Monet, in works such as *Vase of Peonies* (1882) and *Peony Garden* (1887), Pablo Picasso, with *Peonies* (1901), and Auguste Renoir's Impressionist *Peonies* (1878). *Paeonia officinalis* can be found in the altar picture of Maria im Rosenhag by Schongauer in the former Dominican Church in Colmar, while Giuseppe Castiglione (1688-1766), an Italian Jesuit, painter and architect, painted peonies during his time at the court of the Qianlong Emperor during the Qing dynasty.

Above: *Peonies in a Vase on a Stand* (1845-65), a
still life painting by Édouard Manet, inspired
similar works by other celebrated artists like
Vincent Van Gogh, whose own peonies appear
alongside, top right.

English writer Virginia Woolf greatly admired peonies, mentioning their blooms on several occasions in her correspondence.

The peony in literature

In the ancient Chinese *Book of Odes*, peonies appear as love symbols exchanged between young people and as with visual art the flower features frequently in In English-language poetry, peonies have been utilised with an alternate symbolism that they do for east Asian writers. In traditional Chinese and Japanese art, peonies broadly represent both female beauty, as well as wealth and status. Western poets use peony blossoms to evoke spring, ephemeral beauty and fleeting infatuation.

English writer Virginia Woolf greatly admired peonies, mentioning their blooms on several occasions in her correspondence and making the jovial comment to Saxon Sydney-Turner in June 1919 that 'I don't care how thickly I flatter old gentlemen if they will give me peonies'. There are two examples of them being used symbolically in Woolf's fiction: the first occurs in her 1918 short story 'The Evening Party', where the narrator notes of a stranger in the garden that 'She's touched the peony; all the petals fall'; the second is in her final novel, *Between the Acts*, where the character Bart picks up a 'peony that had shed its petals' while looking back at the country house that provides the setting for the story – on both occasions the peony is used to convey the sudden fading of beauty.

Contemporary British artists

Peonies continue to inspire artists today and we have personally worked with established British artist and illustrator Carolyn Carter (an old school friend of mine), who has used our peonies as inspiration for a fine art collection and beautiful modern giftware range. Carolyn has always loved the dramatic blooms of peonies and is drawn to paint the wonderful tones of their many petals as the light catches them. She hopes to capture the vibrant bursts of colour they display in such intricate and delicate forms.

Opposite page, bottom right: *Hope Blooms* by British artist Carolyn Carter, part of a collection of fine art paintings inspired by peonies.

Above: Peony home and giftware range, designed by Carolyn Carter.

A Reflection of Contemporary Times

Peonies have been bred for centuries and been highly regarded for their beauty, scent and medicinal properties. Throughout the years peonies have always reflected the art, culture and fashion of the times and are still in vogue today. Of particular importance, in a crowded, busy, sometimes hectic lifestyle, peonies can be seen as a beacon of beauty and can provide calm reflection; their longevity reminds us to live in the here and now and appreciate that whilst peony plants may remain constant and endure in the garden, we should treasure every fleeting, flowering moment.

1851 *Paeonia lactiflora* 'Festiva Maxima' AGM (Miellez, 1851)

A wonderful double white, beautifully scented mid-season flowering peony. Hugely popular for over 150 years and an excellent cut flower that is widely used in bridal bouquets today.

1856 *Paeonia lactiflora* 'Duchessee de Nemours' AGM (Calot, 1856)

One of the most popular white and fragrant early to mid-season flowering peonies. Named after Marie d'Orléans-Longueville, Duchesse de Nemours (1625-1707). Despite being in commercial production for over 150 years, this peony remains a firm favourite as a cut flower.

1906 *Paeonia lactiflora* 'Sarah Bernhardt' AGM (Lemoine, 1906)

Named after Sarah Bernhardt (1844-1923), a popular and successful actress who was a pioneer in sound recordings and motion pictures. This peony is hands down one of the most popular and highly regarded peonies in the world today and makes an outstanding cut flower.

1952   *Paeonia lactiflora* **'Shirley Temple' AGM (from Holland, before 1952)**

This wonderful double white peony opens blush-pink, changing to pure white as the bloom matures, and is named after Shirley Temple (1928-2014), American child star, actress and singer and legend of classic Hollywood.

1964   *Paeonia* **'Coral Charm' AGM (Wissing, 1964)**

An early to mid-season flowering peony that is very special because of its beautiful coral colour. Although introduced in 1964, this peony has steadily increased in popularity with gardeners and noticeably since 2019, when Living Coral was named Pantone® colour of the year, reflecting the growing fashion for pastel and especially coral colours.

2002   *Paeonia* **'Singing in the Rain' (Smith, 2002)**

A floriferous and striking semi-double mid-season flowering peony with yellow flowers suffused with pink, giving the appearance of a pale orange colour. This peony was named by Smith for remaining upright and unaffected by a rain storm the night before a garden tour. *Singing in the Rain* was a very popular 1952 musical romantic comedy, often considered to be one of the greatest films of all time.

Places to see Peonies

Woburn Abbey & Gardens, Bedfordshire

Bedfordshire has been the home of the Earls and Dukes of Bedford since the 1620s. It is currently the home of the 15th Duke and his family. The 30-acre gardens were designed by landscape designer Humphry Respton in 1752. There are peonies in the four long borders not far from the Chinese Dairy.

Knebworth House & Gardens, Hertfordshire

A historic Hertfordshire house in Knebworth and home to the Lyttons since 1490, its 28-acre garden was created in the 17th century. Peonies can be found in the herb garden, amongst the Malus Walk and also in the herbaceous borders near the roses.

Fenton House, London

A 17th-century London house in Hampstead village which now belongs to the National Trust, bequeathed to them in 1952 by Lady Binning. The two-acre garden is laid out over three levels and peonies can be found in the borders of the main walled garden.

Osterley Park and House, London

This Georgian country estate in West London, built in 1761 by Robert Adam and passed to the National Trust in 1991, was used for the filming of the 2021 film *The Dark Knight Rises*. The 18th-century landscape park comprises 350 acres, with the peonies located in the Tudor walled garden and the flower garden.

Boarstall Tower, Buckinghamshire

Now a National Trust property, this 14th-century moated gatehouse has around three acres of beautiful gardens. There are vibrant peonies in the large borders close by to the gatehouse.

Hodnet Hall, Shropshire

Situated in Drayton, Shropshire, Hodnet Hall was built in 1870 and is owned by the Heber-Percy family. The 63-acre garden was developed in 1921 by Brigadier Algernon Heber-Percy, a keen landscape gardener, and is now considered one of the best examples of a planted landscape in Britain.

Englefield House and Gardens, Berkshire

An Elizabethan country house with surrounding estate in Englefield, Berkshire. Owned by Richard Fellowes Benyon, the house has 19th and 20th-century formal terraced gardens, as well as water and woodland gardens, totalling five hectares. The peonies are in the borders by the stone balustrades and staircase on the lower terraces.

Hatfield House and Gardens, Hertfordshire

A large Jacobean country house built in 1611 by Robert Cecil, chief minister to King James I, It is now owned by Robert Gascoyne-Cecil, 7th Marquess of Salisbury. With over 40 acres of gardens, including a great Jacobean garden, peonies can be found in the Sundial Garden, Viewing Bay and the Old Palace Garden.

Penshurst Place and Gardens, Kent

A 14th-century manor house with 11 acres of formal gardens. The house, once the property of King Henry VIII, was left to his son King Edward VI and granted to Sir William Sidney later in 1552. The Sidney family still occupy the house today. There is a spectacular 100-metre-long peony border near The Orchard.

Wrest Park, Bedfordshire

A country estate with a Grade I listed house and gardens in Silsoe, Bedfordshire, Wrest Park belonged to the powerful de Grey family, Earls of Kent from 1280, and was acquired by English Heritage in 2006. The 90-acre gardens are a mixture of three distinct gardening styles from 1700-1850. You will find the peonies in the borders of the walled garden.

Spetchley Park Estate & Gardens, Worcestershire

Located near Worcester, this Grade II listed house and park have been in the Berkeley family for over 400 years. The gardens and park were developed over this period, most notably by Ellen Willmott, the sister of Rose Berkeley, in the late 19th and early 20th centuries.

Mill Dene Garden, Gloucestershire

Established in 1965 in Moreton-in-Marsh, Gloucester, this 2.5-acre garden surrounds a Cotswold watermill. Owned by Wendy Dare, with the help of Rubert Golby they have designed a highly individual garden with different types of peonies throughout.

Docwra's Manor Garden, Cambridgeshire

Parts of Docwra's Manor in Royston, Cambridgeshire date back to the 15th century. Owner Faith Raven has developed an orchard, a paved garden and a walled garden, where you will find the peonies.

Kiftsgate Court, Gloucestershire

Built in 1887 and perched on the edge of the Cotswolds above the village of Mickleton is Kiftsgate Court, owned by the Chambers family. There have been three generations of women gardeners at Kiftsgate, started by Heather Muir in the 1920s, continued by Diany Binny from 1950 and now looked after by Anne Chambers and her husband. The garden, around two hectares, is in tiers. The first tier has the majority of peonies, with a few located on the bottom tier.

Waterperry House and Gardens, Oxfordshire

Near Oxford, this house was built in 1713 and sold to Oxford University in 1925, then to Miss Beatrix Havergal 1932 and finally to the School of Philosophy & Economic Science. The eight acres of beautifully landscaped gardens have many different sections, with peonies in the herbaceous border and virgin walk.

Sussex Prairie Garden, Sussex

Britain's largest prairie (eight acres) is found in the heart of Sussex in Henfield. The borders at the front of the large main garden have many peonies and tree peonies can be found in the small garden by the house. Owned by Paul and Pauline McBride, the garden was based on the world-renowned Dutch landscape designer Piet Oudolf.

Loseley Park, Surrey

Built in 1560 during the reign of Elizabeth I, Loseley Park stands in ancient Surrey parkland close to the North Downs. Still the home of the More-Molyneux family, it is still remarkably unchanged since 1562, when Sir William More laid the first stones. The 2.5-acre walled garden was designed by Gertrude Jekyll, while the peonies are in the White Garden.

Highdown Gardens, Sussex

On the western edge of Worthing, West Sussex, from 1909 these gardens overlooking the sea were owned by Sir Frederick and Lady Sybil Stern, who purchased and swapped thousands of seeds and cuttings from around the world, including China, which is why there is a huge collection of tree peonies here. With this unique pedigree, Highdown Gardens was recognised as a national Plant Collection in 1989 by Plant Heritage.
The middle garden has peonies, but the most spectacular are the very mature large tree peonies in the lower garden.

Index

Acknowledgements

I had no idea how big a project this would turn out to be and that it would involve the hard work and dedication of quite so many people. This book is the result of a team effort and it is humbling to realise how many people have been involved in producing it.

The book has been more than four years in the planning and execution, not least because our window of opportunity to take the photographs of peonies in flower was only a few months each year and naturally coincided with our busiest time on the nursery and whilst we were away at flower shows. Of course, the global pandemic provided further challenges but did at least allow some time to concentrate on the book. The whole process has been hard work but I have found it enjoyable and very rewarding and I am most grateful to all involved for their continual support and enthusiasm throughout this lengthy process. Whilst I have done my best to ensure accuracy, any error, inaccuracies or omissions are entirely my own and are part of my continuing learning journey.

This book is dedicated to my grandparents, who shared their love and joy of gardening with me and instilled in me a deep and enduring love of nature, the outdoors and growing plants. I am especially grateful for their continued love, encouragement and guidance whilst I have pursued my passion.

The photographs in this book are incredible and they have taken a huge amount of effort to produce. I wanted the book to show peonies in context in gardens and landscapes, not just as close-up images (although the close-up pictures are sensational), and it was always important to me that the book contained inspirational photographs. In particular, I must thank Caron Saunders, who has spent the past few years liaising with lots of private and public homes and gardens and chasing around the English countryside, usually at very short notice, to photograph peonies during the few days while each of the plants were in bloom. Caron has also taken many of the photographs of peonies on our nursery and her enthusiasm for this project has been motivating for all of us there. I must also thank Bronwynne Britt, Lauren Harper and Abbie Pearce for the photographs they have taken at flower shows and on the nursery. Over the past few years we have put together photo shoots to produce awe-inspiring images of peonies here at the nursery. I am grateful to our model, Jodie Francis, who has worked with us for many of these photo shoots and has calmly and professionally (and always with a smile) climbed into cold baths filled with peonies in the middle of our field, worn ridiculously heavy headdresses at Chelsea and been pictured with our alpacas and, on one occasion, a skittish racehorse. Our commercial photographers, Jodie Morris and Steve Fisher, must also be given my grateful thanks and due recognition for the amazing photographs they have taken on our photo shoots. My thanks to photographers Clive Nichols and Richard Bloom for photographing peonies at the nursery and for allowing us to use images of theirs taken at private homes and gardens must also be recorded. Their images are extraordinary and moving and the book would not be complete without them. All of the photographs that are out of focus and poorly framed are, of course, mine.

Carolyn Carter is an amazing artist and her work is simply breathtaking. I have always admired Carolyn's work, even whilst we were at school together, and I have been delighted and honoured that she has agreed to work with the nursery over the past few years, designing our giftware range, producing sketches of our Chelsea exhibits, creating beautiful paintings of peonies and painting the illustrations in the book. Carolyn is one of England's finest artistic talents and I am so incredibly grateful that she has worked with me on this project.

The importance of my parents to my story cannot be underestimated. Their support and guidance has been unwavering, especially when I chose to change careers and pursue my dream to grow plants.

My parents co-own the nursery and I work alongside them every day; I am grateful that we are able to spend so much time together. Both my parents are instrumental in attending and building our flower show exhibits and, in recent years, whilst my children are young, have covered flower shows so that I may stay at home and also have provided childcare when I have been needed at the nursery. My parents have worked tirelessly in support of my ambitions and I am truly thankful for their love and encouragement.

I must thank my fellow flower show exhibitors for their generosity and advice, especially in relation to feedback on exhibits and coping with the stresses of exhibiting around the country. My exhibits have sometimes been challenging and it has been a real comfort to have such friends and colleagues around. On the subject of challenging exhibits, my thanks go to Andy Willison, a great friend and talented designer and event florist.

My thanks are due to my publishers, Graffeg, in particular to Peter Gill and designers David Williams and Joana Rodrigues and editor Daniel Williams, for their dedication, patience, advice and guidance during what has been a long and complicated process. I am so excited by what we have achieved together, thank you.

There are two people without whom this book would not exist. Bronwynne Britt and Angela Oliver have been incredible friends and colleagues. Angela's belief in me and in my dreams is uplifting and sustains me. I am also grateful for the supply of morning pastries. Bronwynne has been by my side from the very beginning of this project and has provided invaluable advice and guidance, tirelessly pushing and encouraging me. Their kindness, support and friendship has given me the courage to undertake this project and to see it through. I am forever indebted.

My final thanks must go to my family. My wife, Emma, and three children, Henry, Monty and Persephone, have been and continue to be amazing and a constant source of pride and pleasure to me. Their indulgence and patience as I pursue my passion is awesome, as I spend so much time away from home either at the nursery or at flower shows. To my wife, simply, thank you for your constant support and love. To my children, thank you for your understanding and enthusiasm; I would encourage you to follow your own path in life, be happy and pursue your own dreams, whatever they may be (spaceman, ninja and princess are all valid careers) because it has been a dream come true for me to grow peonies.